THE SKELETON AND MOVEMENT

Revised Edition

Steve Parker

Series Consultant
Dr Alan Maryon-Davis
MB, BChir, MSc, MRCP, FFCM

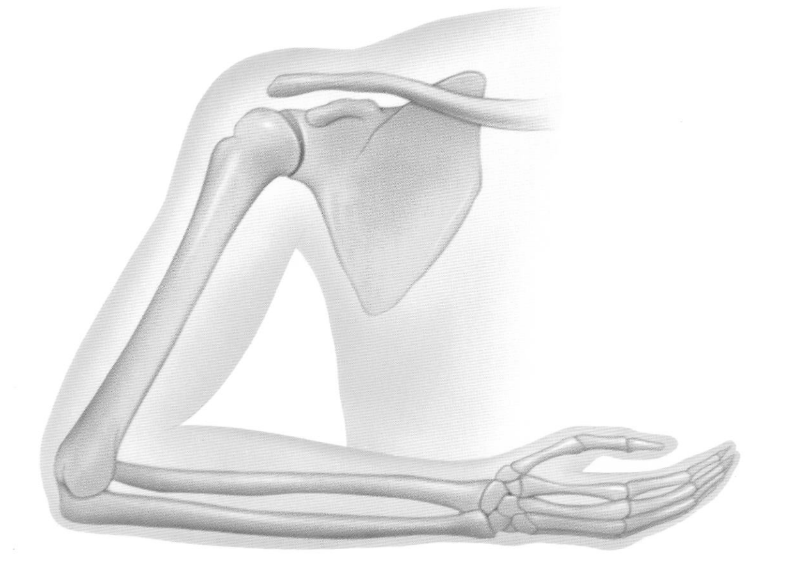

Franklin Watts
New York • Chicago • London • Toronto • Sydney

Original edition first published in 1981

Franklin Watts Inc.
95 Madison Avenue
New York, NY 10016

ISBN 0-531-10709-4 (lib.)/ISBN 0-531-24606-X (pbk.)

Library of Congress Catalog Card Number: 88-51608

Illustrations: Andrew Aloof, Marion Appleton, Howard Dyke, David Mallott, Mick Saunders, Roy Wiltshire

Photographs: Clark Robinson Ltd (with thanks to The Backstore, London) 15; Science Photo Library 13; Science Photo Library: Michael Abbey 45; CNRI 11, 12, 18, 19; Eric Grave 27, 45; Dr Howells 9; Manfred Kage cover; James Stevenson 35; Zefa Picture Library 23, 28, 32, 36, 41, 43.

All illustrations are from the original edition

Printed in Belgium

Contents

The human skeleton

Imagine a human body without its bones. It would be a wobbly heap, unable to stand up or move. The bones provide support and shape for the **muscles**, nerves and other soft parts of the body. They are also a system of rigid levers, which the muscles can pull against to move parts of the body.

All the bones together are called the **skeleton**. There is a central column, the backbone or **spine**, with a skull at the head end and a "tail" at the other end. Towards each end of the backbone there are two limbs, which are attached to the spine by broad, flat bones called limb girdles. The human skeleton has the same basic design as the skeleton of many other animals with backbones (vertebrates) – from mice to elephants.

The adult human skeleton consists of about 206 bones. A baby has more than 300 bones, but some of them join together during growth. As we develop, each bone grows to the right shape for the job it has to do. At the point where one bone meets another, there is a **joint**. Some joints allow a lot of movement; others only slight movement.

Apart from movement, the skeleton also carries out other functions. Inside some bones is a jelly-like substance, bone **marrow**, which makes new blood **cells**. Bones store body minerals like **calcium**, which can be released if they are needed elsewhere in the body. Parts of the skeleton protect the soft, delicate organs within them. The skull protects the brain, and the ribs form a strong cage around the heart and lungs.

Names of bones

Every bone in the body has a special scientific name, which is used by people such as doctors and biologists. Some bones also have common names:

Scientific name	Common name
carpals	wrist bones
clavicle	collar bone
mandible	lower jaw
maxilla	upper jaw
patella	knee cap
pelvis	hip bone
radius, ulna	forearm bones
sternum	breastbone
tarsals	ankle bones
tibia	shin bone
femur	thigh bone
vertebrae	spine or backbone

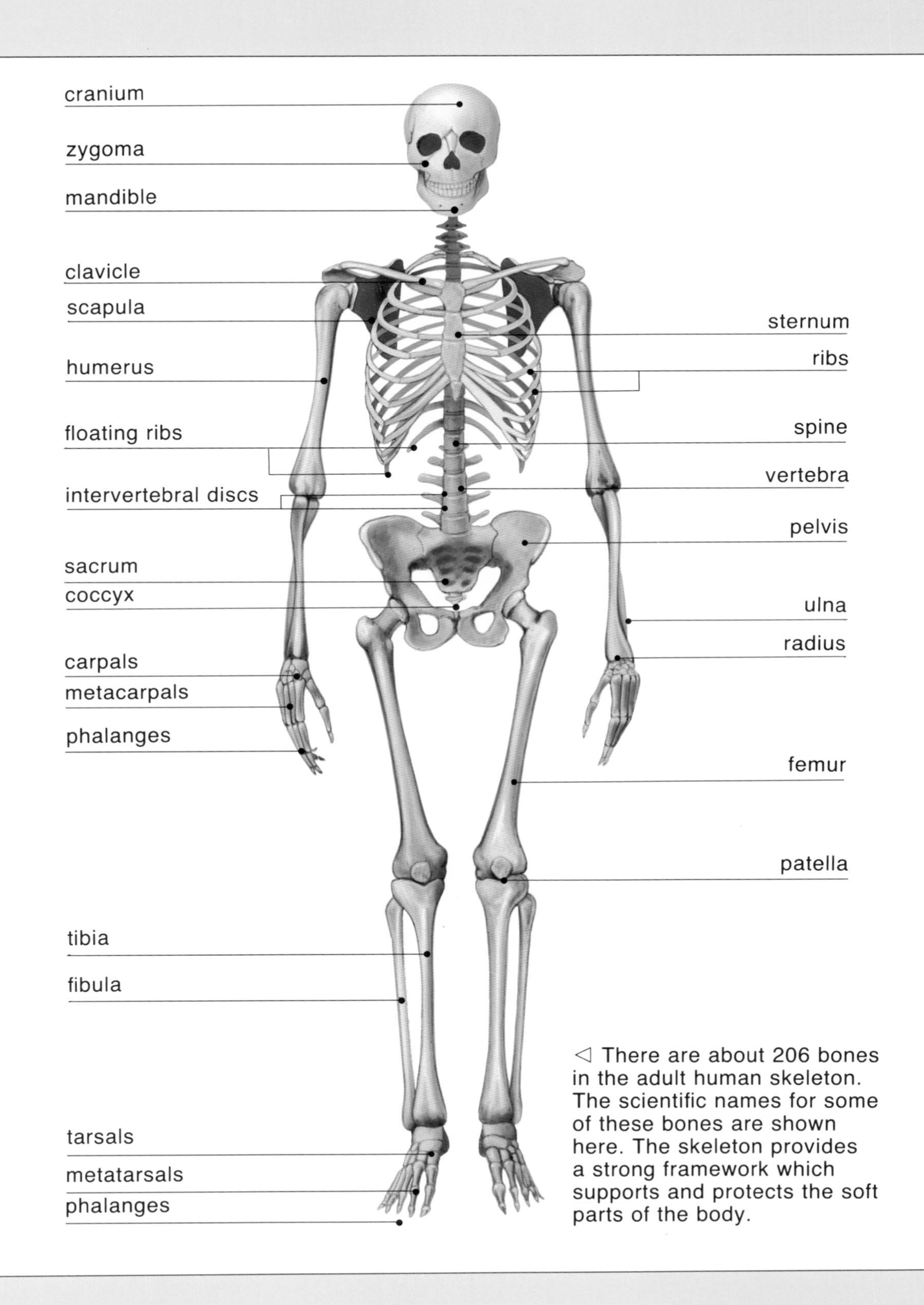

◁ There are about 206 bones in the adult human skeleton. The scientific names for some of these bones are shown here. The skeleton provides a strong framework which supports and protects the soft parts of the body.

Movement

Bones

- The smallest bones in the human body are three tiny bones called the hammer (malleus), anvil (incus) and stirrup (stapes) inside each ear (see page 12).
- The largest bone is the thigh bone (**femur**). It makes up nearly one-quarter of a person's height.
- Without regular exercise, bones lose their minerals and become weaker.

We can move because bones and muscles work together, under the control of the brain. The entire process of making a movement is complicated, yet it can happen in a split second.

The brain receives messages from the sense organs and coordinates these signals with brain areas involved with movement. It then sends messages along nerves to the correct muscles. The nerve messages make the muscles shorten (contract) and so move the bones. The sensory organs send information to the brain regarding the success of the movement, and whether another movement is required.

◁ The skeleton is rigid, yet flexible at the same time. Joints between the bones allow them to move in relation to each other. The skeleton is one main part of the musculo-skeletal system.

A movement usually involves dozens of muscles. If you stand up and raise your arm, many muscles in your arm, neck, shoulder and back are working together in a coordinated manner. Other muscles in your back and legs adjust your body posture so that you keep your balance. Balancing is one of many movements which are carried out all the time without our being aware of them. It involves specialized sensors within the muscles which tell the brain how stretched they are. These are called **proprioceptors**.

Complicated movements, like playing the piano, need a lot of concentration and practice at first. The brain must organize the muscles and bones to make the right movements at the right times. When the basic technique has been learned, it is then repeated over and over again, so that less time is spent thinking about the movements themselves and more time can be given to improving the technique.

Muscles

- There are about 650 muscles concerned with moving parts of the body. These are called skeletal muscles.
- The smallest muscles are attached to the smallest bones, which are in the ear.
- The largest muscles are the gluteus muscles in the buttocks, which move the legs.
- Muscles, like bones, need regular use to keep them healthy. Without exercise, they become flabby and waste away.

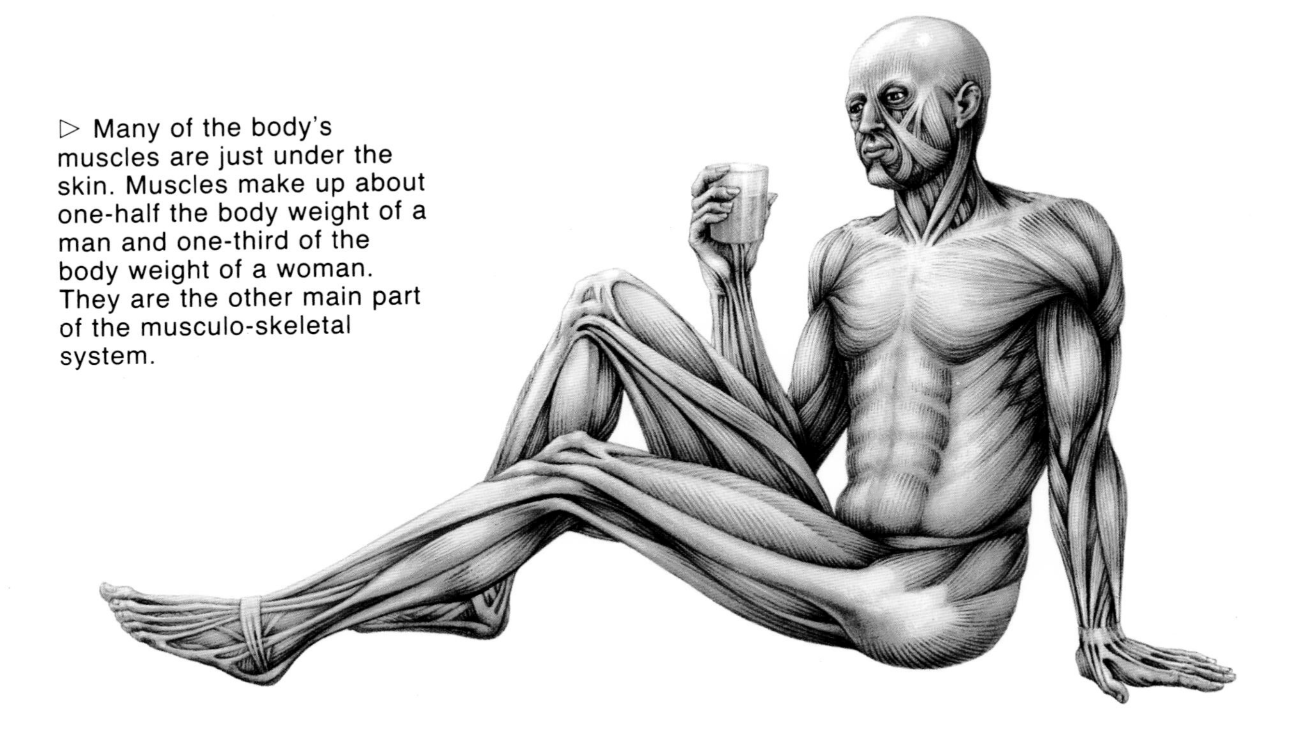

▷ Many of the body's muscles are just under the skin. Muscles make up about one-half the body weight of a man and one-third of the body weight of a woman. They are the other main part of the musculo-skeletal system.

Bone structure

Changing bone

Because bone is a living, growing tissue, it responds to extra stresses by growing. It is possible to guess a person's type of job or leisure pursuit from the size and shape of their bones. Peoples who spend a lot of time riding horses may develop thicker thigh bones than normal, and some of the muscles and tendons in their thighs and calves become stiffened and hardened by a bone-like substance.

Keeping bones healthy

Besides regular exercise, a healthy diet is needed to keep bones in good condition. Calcium and vitamin D are especially important.

- Astronauts and people who stay in bed lose calcium and other minerals from their bodies.
- Some older people, especially women, develop osteoporosis or "brittle bones." In this condition, collagen is lost and the bones break more easily. Regular exercise helps to prevent the disease from developing.

Bone is very well designed for its job. It is strong, yet light. The skeleton makes up only about one-seventh of the weight of the whole body. It has a tensile or "stretching" strength almost as strong as cast iron, but is only one-third of the weight. For its weight, bone is stronger than steel or reinforced concrete.

Living bone is very different from the dry, flaky bones you can see in museums. About one-fifth of the weight of bone is water. More than 50 per cent of bone's weight is made up of minerals, like calcium, magnesium, carbonate and phosphate, which gives it hardness. One-third of bone consists of organic material, mainly **collagen**. Collagen is a tough, fibrous substance which gives bone a certain amount of elasticity. This slightly flexible nature is one reason for bone's great strength. To absorb strain, bone can bend a little, instead of snapping.

Bone cells, which are visible only under the microscope, lie in holes within the hard bone. They have fine, thread-like extensions that pass through tiny canals in the bone to join with other cells. The holes occupied by the bone cells are arranged in rings around larger canals, called Haversian canals. These run parallel to the length of the bone and contain blood vessels. A hard outer wall of bone surrounds these structures, and a tough, stringy sheath, the **periosteum**, is wrapped like a "skin" around the whole bone. This contains blood vessels and nerves.

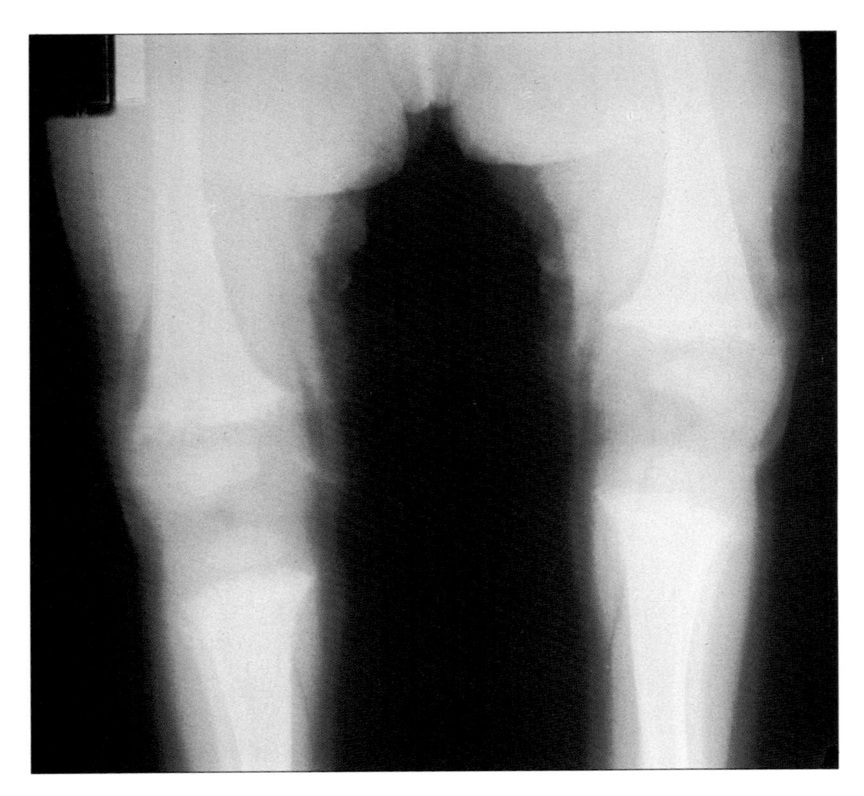

◁ X-ray pictures show only hard parts of the body, such as bones, in white. This picture shows the short, bent bones in the legs of a child with the disease **rickets**. This is caused by a lack of vitamin D, which makes the bones become soft and misshapen.

▽ This cutaway diagram shows the various parts inside a bone (in this case, the top end of the thigh bone). Like other parts of the body, bone has a good supply of blood vessels and nerves.

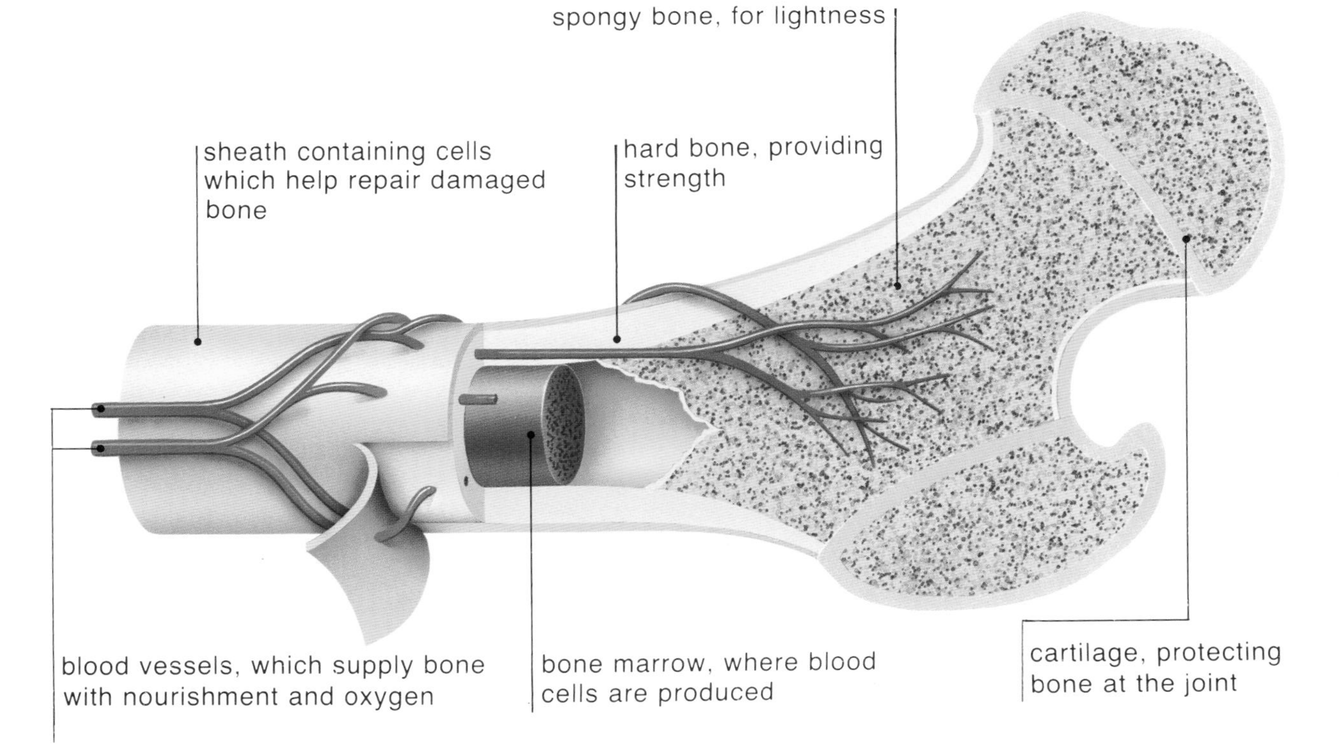

Connective tissue

▽ A view of the tendons, ligaments and cartilage in the knee joint, from the side (below) and the front (below right). They are all types of connective tissue. Connective tissue is made of cells which form a sort of rubbery jelly around themselves. In this jelly are various kinds of fibers.

The various parts of the musculo-skeletal system are joined together. Muscles are joined to bones and bones are joined to other bones. Three main types of connective tissue – **tendons, ligaments** and **cartilage** – help the parts of the system to work together.

Tendons are tough, stringy "ropes," which join muscles to bones. Many muscles taper to strong, rope-like tendons at each end. The tendon must pass on the pull of a muscle to the bone without

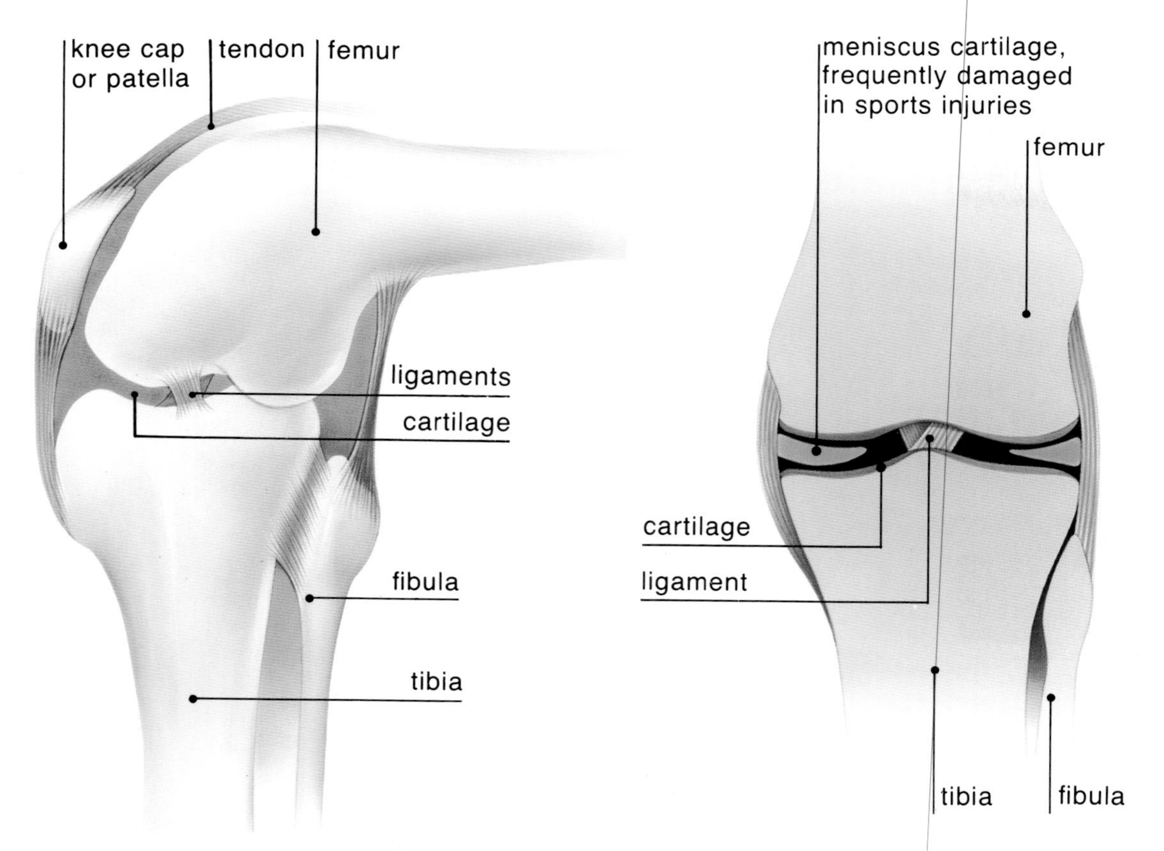

tearing itself. When we walk or run, the tendons in the calf and the arch of the foot stretch slightly and then spring back to their original length. This means the muscles do not have to work so hard and saves energy. Ligaments are strong fibrous "straps," which holds bones together at joints. They give stability to a joint, so that the bones can move without coming apart completely.

Cartilage is the body's "rubber." It is a type of connective tissue associated with the skeleton and is a flexible, gristly substance which supports and protects various parts of the body. When a baby develops, the "bones" appear first as cartilage. As the baby grows, most of this cartilage hardens into bone. Cartilage remains at the ends of the bones, around the joints.

▽ This X-ray of the shoulder shows the main bones. The large ball at the top end of the upper-arm bone (**humerus**) is on the lower left. The girder-like collar bone (**clavicle**) runs from center top down to the right. The shoulder blade (**scapula**) is the faint, wide bone on the right. Ligaments, seen as light blue all around the joint, hold these large bones in position.

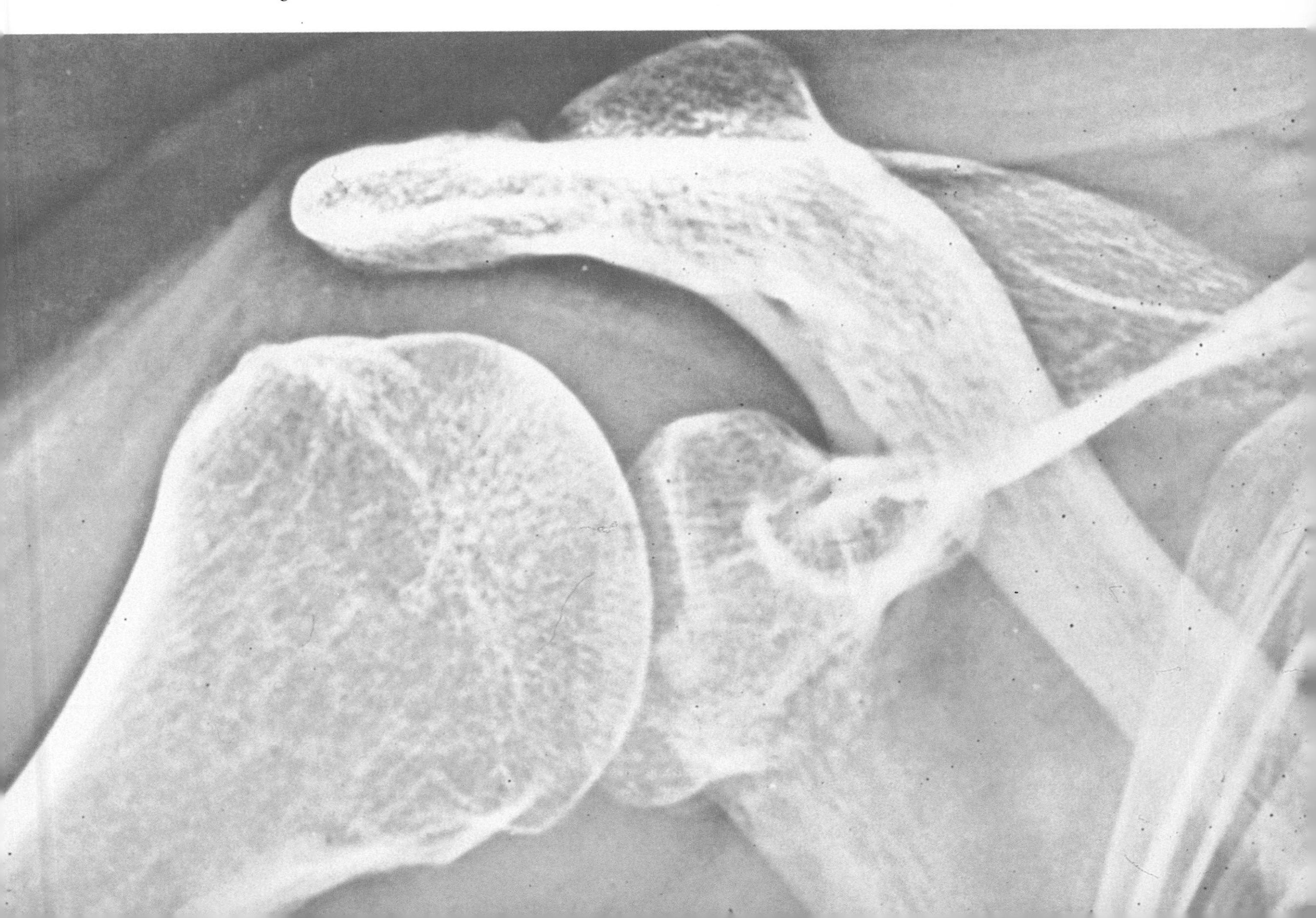

The skull

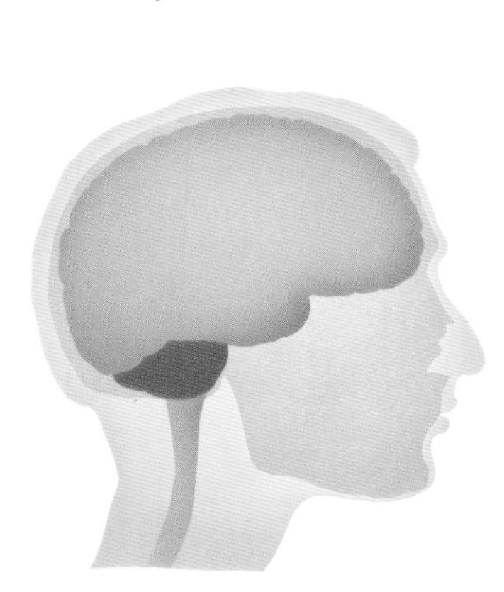

△ The brain takes up the main part of the skull, the hollow cranium. Between the brain and the skull bone are shock-absorbing layers of tissue and fluid.

▽ The skull houses the smallest bones in the body, the three tiny bones inside each ear (page 6). They form a system of levers which pass sound vibrations from the air to the inner ear.

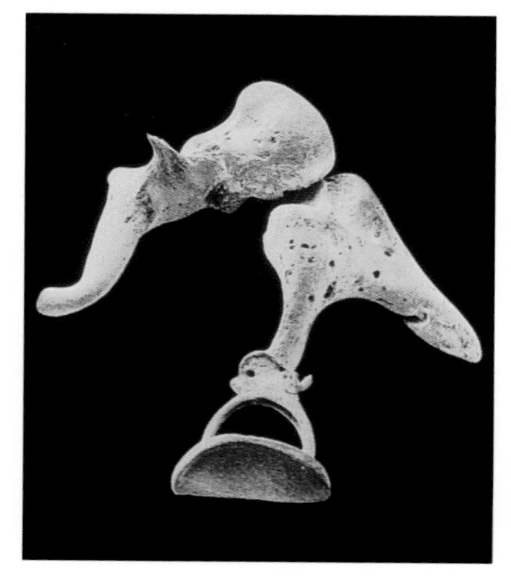

Inside the head, the human skull balances on top of the spine like an egg on a pole. In fact the skull, like an eggshell, is surprisingly strong, given its thinness. Its curved design resists squashing and squeezing from various directions. The skull contains and protects the eyes, the ears, the mouth and teeth, the nose and the most vital organ of all, the brain.

The main part of the skull is the **cranium**, or "brainbox," which protects the brain. It is made of eight separate bones, tightly joined together by zig-zag joints called **sutures**. In a baby, these bones are not fully formed and the zig-zag joints are not closed. This allows the cranium to collapse slightly as the baby is born, to help the head to squeeze through the narrow birth canal. By the time the baby is about two years old, the bones have grown and joined together.

At the front of the skull there are fourteen bones, which form the face. Within two large hollows, the eye sockets, the eyeballs swivel up and down and from side to side. The hole in the middle of the face opens into a large cavity, the nasal cavity. The nose itself is not made of bone but of softer, more springy cartilage.

The only part of the skull which can move is the lower jaw. The muscles that move it are anchored to the cheek bones and sides of the skull. Teeth are set into the upper and lower jaws; they are covered with enamel, which is the hardest material in the body – even harder than bone.

▷ The gaps between the bones of the skull show clearly in this X-ray picture of a developing baby. The gap at the top is called the fontanel. It can be felt gently in a newborn baby.

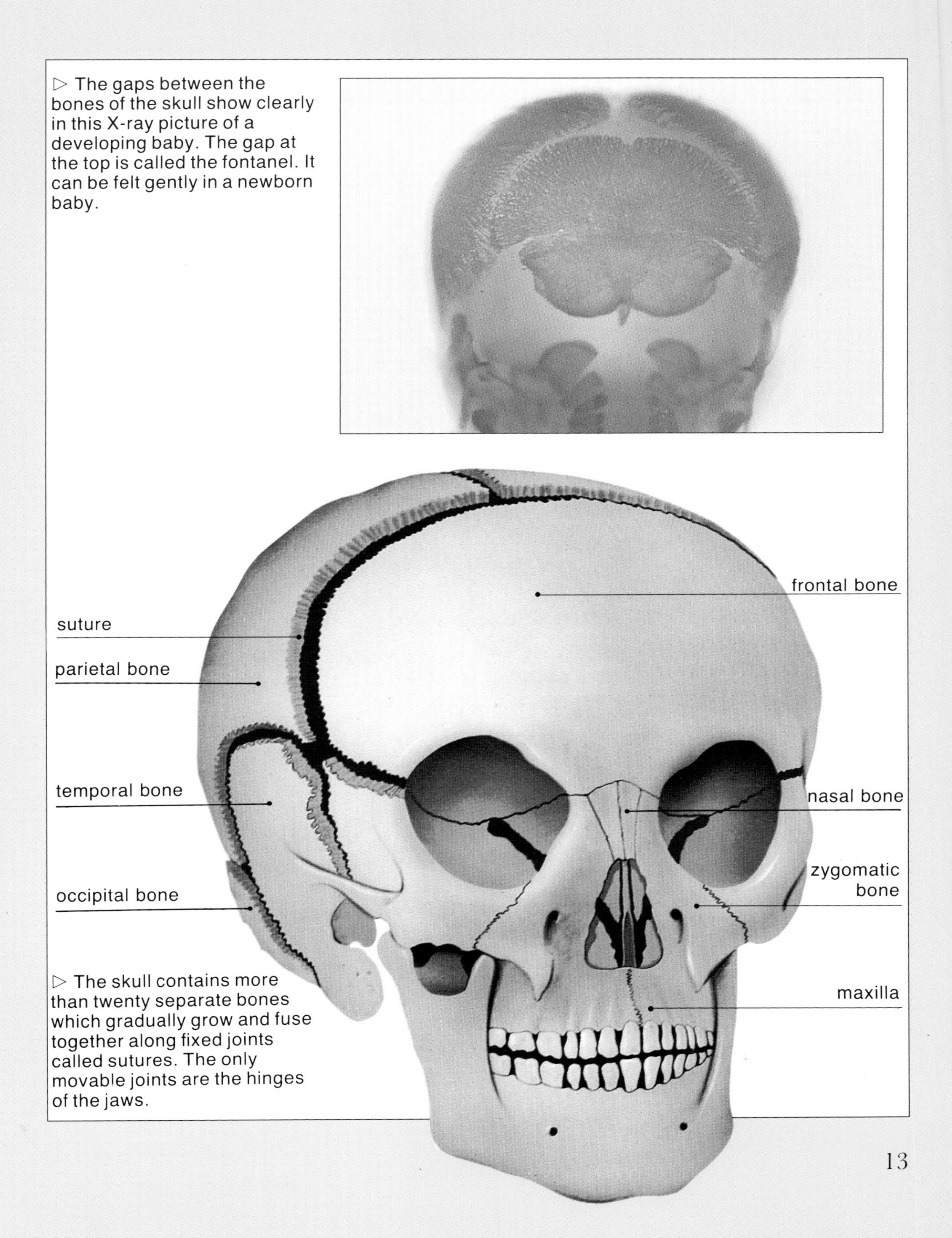

▷ The skull contains more than twenty separate bones which gradually grow and fuse together along fixed joints called sutures. The only movable joints are the hinges of the jaws.

The body's backbone

The spine is truly the body's "backbone." This strong, rod-like collection of 33 bones, called **vertebrae**, supports the main parts of the body in an upright position.

The spine is flexible, to allow us to bend, twist and absorb the stresses of running, lifting and pushing. It is also elastic, to absorb the shocks of walking and running and forms a long, bony tube which protects the **spinal cord**. Nerves passing along the spinal cord connect the brain to the nervous system in the rest of the body.

Each vertebra has a round section at the front, a hole in the middle (through which the spinal cord passes) and bony spikes on each side and at the back. Ligaments and muscles are joined to the spikes, holding the vertebrae together and allowing the back muscles to support and move the entire spine. Between most pairs of vertebrae are washer-like pads of cartilage called **intervertebral disks** (see page 35).

Several other bones join on to the spine. The ribs join on to the twelve vertebrae in the chest region, forming the rib cage. In the hip region, five vertebrae are fused together to make one large bone, the **sacrum**. At the base of the spine is the human "tail," the **coccyx**. It is made of four tiny bones which do not form fully until adulthood. As far as we know, the coccyx has no real use in the body. It may be an evolutionary leftover from prehistoric times, when our ancestors were monkey-like and had long tails.

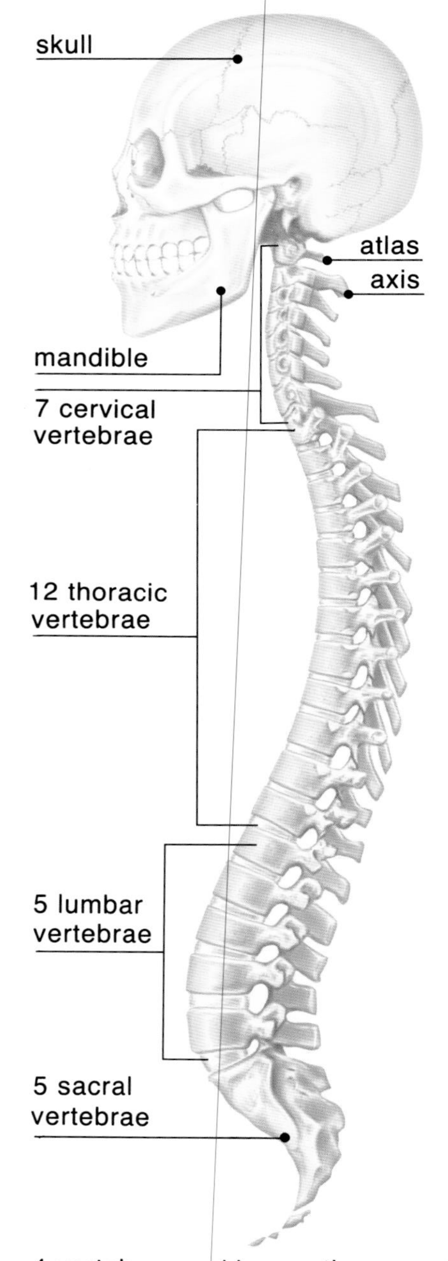

▷ A round-shouldered, slumped-forward sitting position (near right) is bad for your back. Try to sit upright, keeping your back straight, with good support for your lower back and with your head evenly balanced. Specially designed stools (far right) encourage you to sit properly and help to prevent back trouble.

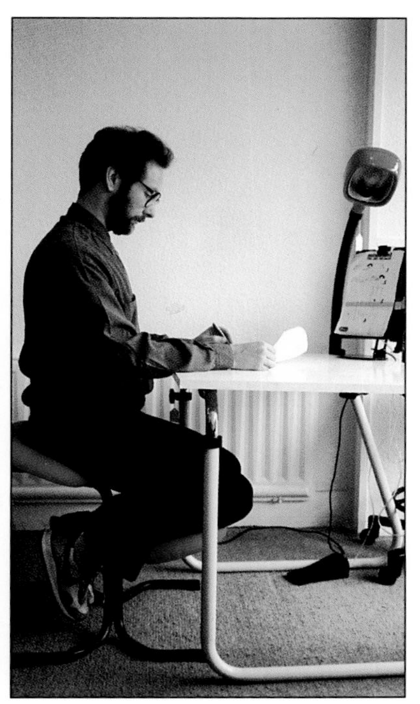

▽ The spinal cord runs along a tunnel formed by the holes through each vertebra. Muscles and ligaments are attached to spikes of bone on either side and to the rear of each vertebra. Two smaller "pegs" of bone face upward and interlock with the next vertebra.

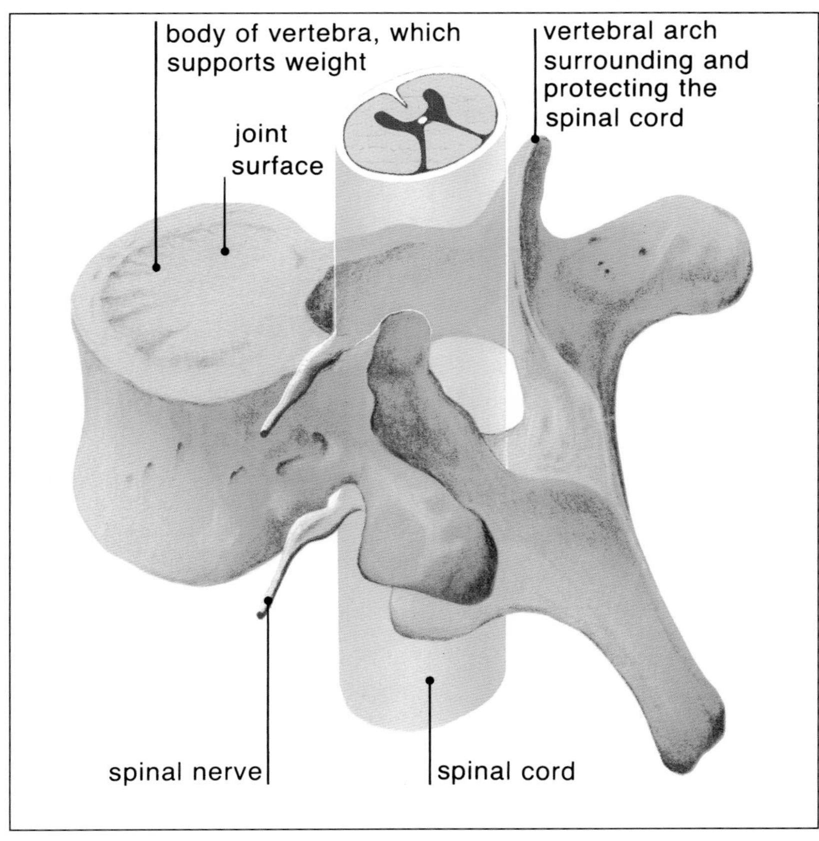

Bad backs

Backache and other kinds of back trouble are a widespread problem. In many countries they are one of the biggest causes of days away from work. Around nine out of ten bad backs get better within one month. To avoid back trouble, try to stand up straight, use chairs and a bed which support the back well, and learn the correct techniques for bending to lift heavy objects without straining the back.

The rib cage

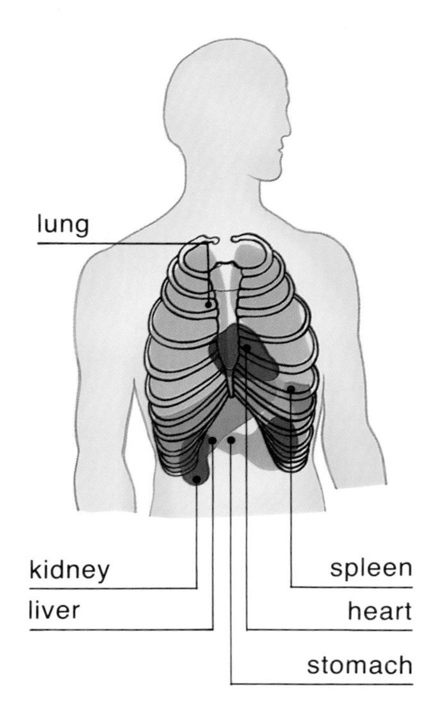

△ The rib cage not only protects the organs inside it (like the heart and lungs); it also extends downward like a shield to cover parts of the kidneys, liver, spleen and stomach.

The human body has twelve pairs of ribs. At the back, each pair is attached to a vertebra. At the front, the top seven pairs are joined to the breastbone (**sternum**) by strips of cartilage called the costal cartilages. They are the true ribs. The other five pairs are called false ribs. The top three pairs of false ribs are joined to the cartilages of the ribs above them. The two lower pairs of ribs have no attachment at the front. They are called floating false ribs.

The ribs themselves are flat, strong, springy bones and the joints at the ends of each rib are flexible. If something hits the chest, the ribs bend and their joints move, to absorb the shock. This prevents the ribs from cracking and damaging the lungs or heart, in all but the most severe injuries.

The ribs provide an anchorage for the muscles and bones of the shoulders and arms. They also form a strong yet flexible cage around the heart, the lungs and the main blood vessels. This allows the lungs to expand as we breathe in and become smaller as we breathe out.

Normal breathing is carried out by the **diaphragm**, a sheet of muscle stretched across the base of the rib cage. As the diaphragm contracts, it flattens and enlarges the chest cavity, sucking in air. As the diaphragm relaxes, it is pushed back into a dome shape by the **abdominal** organs, squeezing air out of the lungs. Deeper breathing involves the whole of the rib cage, as shown on page 17.

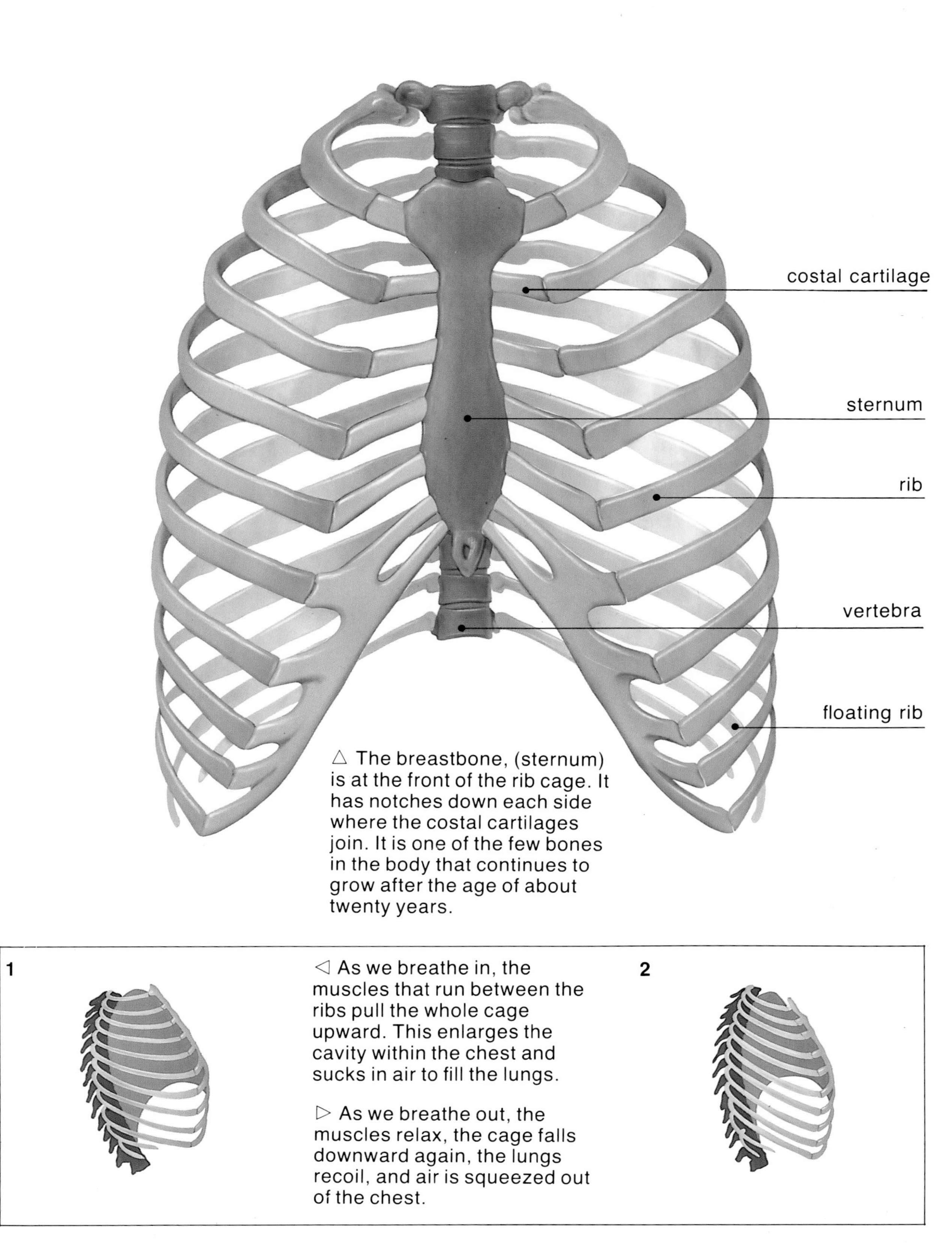

△ The breastbone, (sternum) is at the front of the rib cage. It has notches down each side where the costal cartilages join. It is one of the few bones in the body that continues to grow after the age of about twenty years.

◁ As we breathe in, the muscles that run between the ribs pull the whole cage upward. This enlarges the cavity within the chest and sucks in air to fill the lungs.

▷ As we breathe out, the muscles relax, the cage falls downward again, the lungs recoil, and air is squeezed out of the chest.

Arm and leg bones

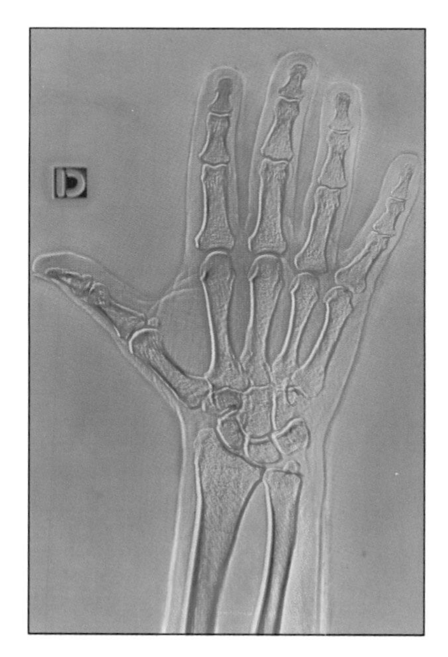

△ The wrist, hand and fingers are made up of many small bones closely joined together. These small bones are capable of very fine movements.

Humans evolved from four-legged ancestors. Four legs, one at each corner of the body, is a stable design for an animal. However, during our evolution, we came to walk upright on two legs. This is less stable, requires good balance, and puts different stresses on the backbone. It did, however, leave our arms free to do other jobs, like gather food, handle tools and use weapons.

Limbs are anchored to the body by large, wide bones, the limb girdles. These are strong enough to take the strain when the arms lift a heavy weight or the legs push off when we jump.

The arm is supported by the shoulder blade (scapula), held in place by many muscles and ligaments. It is braced by the collar bone (clavicle).

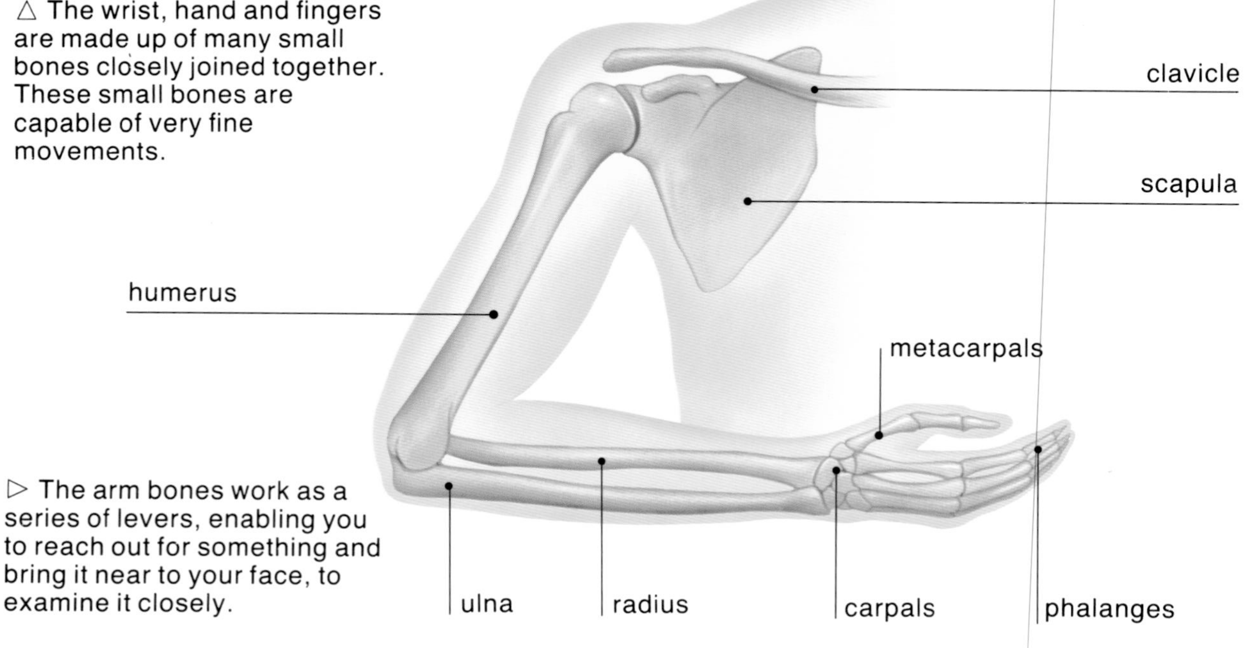

▷ The arm bones work as a series of levers, enabling you to reach out for something and bring it near to your face, to examine it closely.

The upper-arm bone (humerus) is joined to the shoulder blade by a ball-and-socket joint (see page 20). It is extremely mobile – you can swing your arm in a full circle. But it is not all that strong and, under excessive strain in an accident, the two bones occasionally part company. This is called a dislocation.

The leg is attached to the broad, wide hip bone (**pelvis**). The bowl-like shape of the pelvis supports the body, and protects and cradles its contents, such as some of the digestive organs. Like the shoulder, the hip is a ball-and-socket joint. It is less flexible than the shoulder, but much stronger, since it carries a much greater weight.

Broken bones

Despite their strength and good design, bones sometimes break when the stresses on them become too great. A break in a bone is called a fracture. There are several types of fracture.

- In a closed or simple fracture, the bone breaks but the skin does not split. This helps to keep out germs.
- In an open or compound fracture, both skin and bone break, which means there is a danger of germs getting into the wound.
- In a greenstick fracture, the bone splits or cracks like a green twig.
- In a comminuted fracture, the bone splinters or shatters into several pieces.

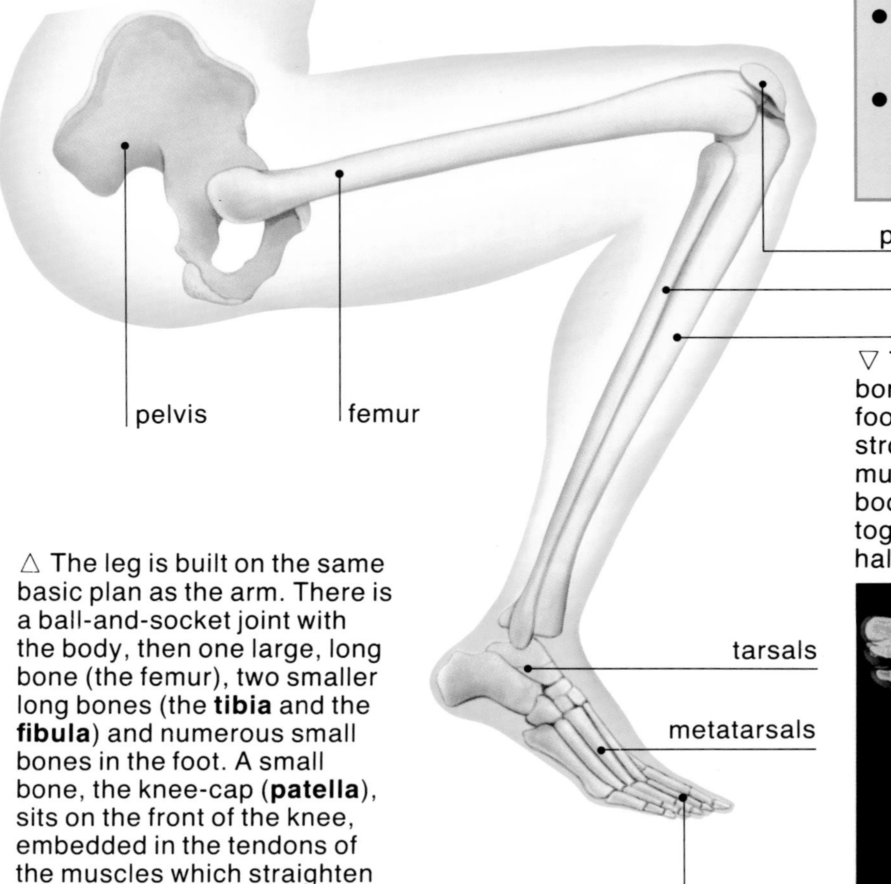

△ The leg is built on the same basic plan as the arm. There is a ball-and-socket joint with the body, then one large, long bone (the femur), two smaller long bones (the **tibia** and the **fibula**) and numerous small bones in the foot. A small bone, the knee-cap (**patella**), sits on the front of the knee, embedded in the tendons of the muscles which straighten the leg.

▽ The foot is made of a set of bones similar to the hand. The foot bones are bigger and stronger, however, since they must carry the weight of the body. The hands and feet together contain more than half of the bones in the body.

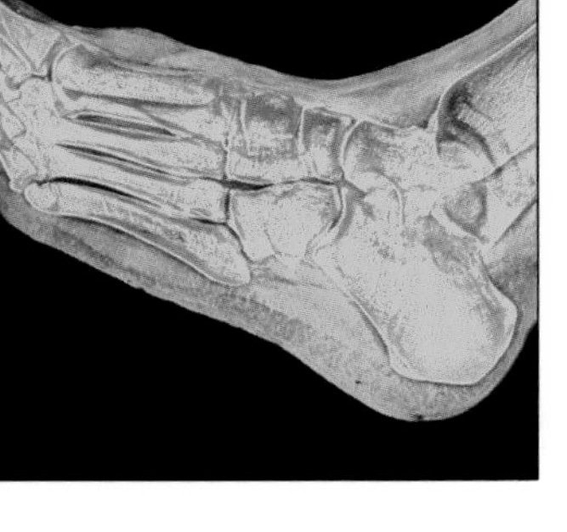

Where bones meet

We can move about because the bones in our skeleton can change position relative to each other. For this to happen, there must be joints between them. A joint is a place where two or more bones meet. There are several kinds of joint in the body; each type helps bones to move in a different way. In this respect, the body is like a complicated machine in which the parts are joined together in different ways, depending on how they are designed to move.

Some "joints" allow no movement at all. Examples are the closely-knit suture joints between the bones of the skull (see page 12). Other joints, such as those between the vertebrae, allow only small movements.

Limb joints, however, allow a wide range of movements, although the bones can only move in certain directions. This is because the joints in the body follow a simple engineering principle – the greater the possible range of movements, the less stable the joint is and the more likely it is to be damaged.

Some joints, like the knuckles, knees and elbows, allow bending only. These are hinge joints. If you try to force this type of joint by twisting it or moving it from side to side, it causes pain.

The size of a joint is also important. The ankle joint and the knee joint (the biggest joint in the body) are larger than their equivalents in the arm, the wrist and elbow. This is because they must carry most of the weight of the body.

▷ Each type of joint allows a certain range of movements, whilst preventing the bones from moving in the wrong direction. These are some of the main types of joint in the body. When disease or wear-and-tear affects certain joints, such as the hip, they may be replaced by artificial joints made of metal or plastics.

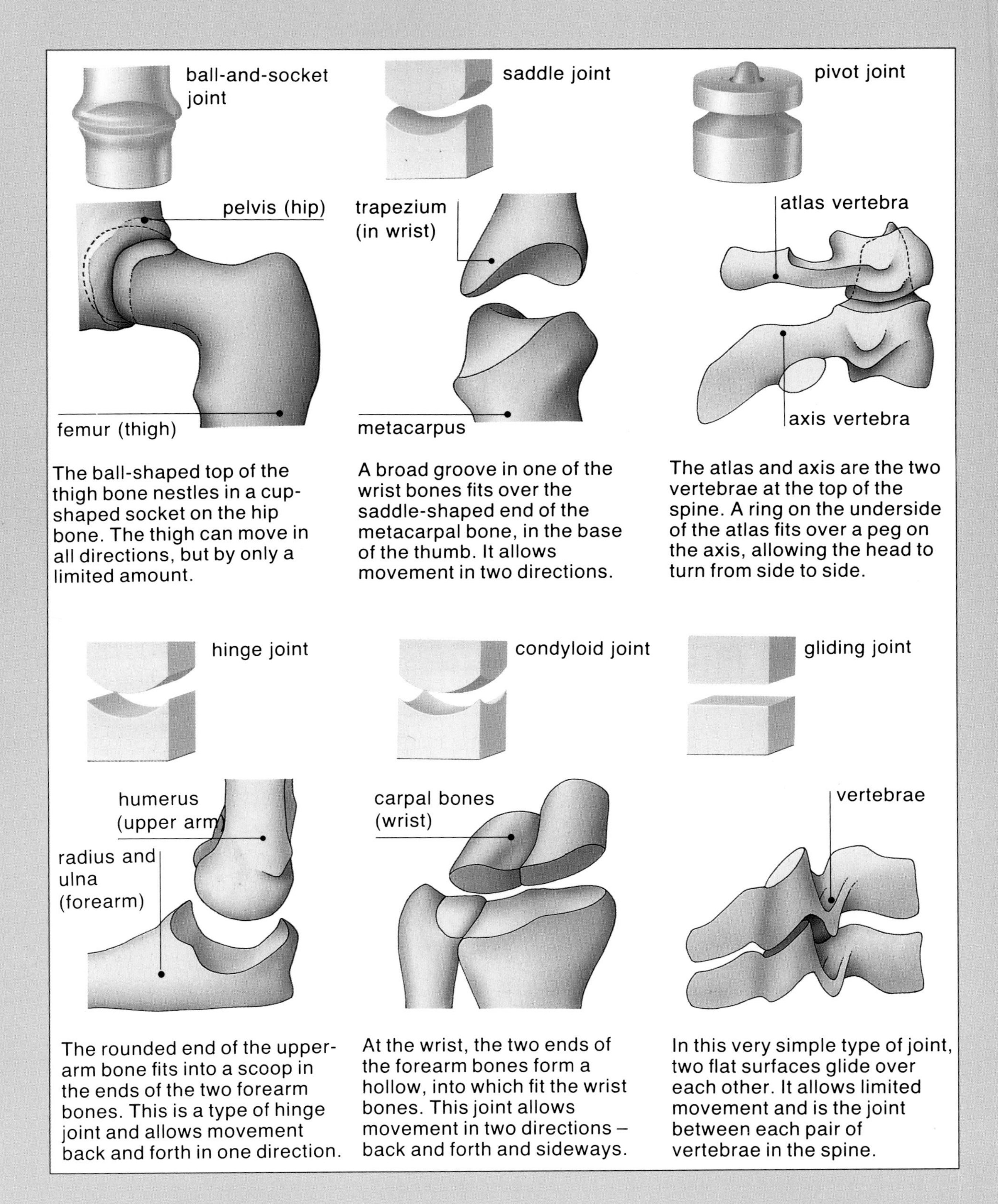

The ball-shaped top of the thigh bone nestles in a cup-shaped socket on the hip bone. The thigh can move in all directions, but by only a limited amount.

A broad groove in one of the wrist bones fits over the saddle-shaped end of the metacarpal bone, in the base of the thumb. It allows movement in two directions.

The atlas and axis are the two vertebrae at the top of the spine. A ring on the underside of the atlas fits over a peg on the axis, allowing the head to turn from side to side.

The rounded end of the upper-arm bone fits into a scoop in the ends of the two forearm bones. This is a type of hinge joint and allows movement back and forth in one direction.

At the wrist, the two ends of the forearm bones form a hollow, into which fit the wrist bones. This joint allows movement in two directions – back and forth and sideways.

In this very simple type of joint, two flat surfaces glide over each other. It allows limited movement and is the joint between each pair of vertebrae in the spine.

Inside a joint

In any machine, the parts that move against each other must be very smooth and well lubricated. A vehicle uses lubricants such as oil and grease for this purpose. There must also be shock absorbers to prevent damage due to the jolting caused by movement.

The joints of the skeleton also have their lubricants and shock absorbers. Each movable joint is enclosed in a bag called the joint capsule. Lining the capsule is a thin layer, the **synovial membrane**. This makes a thick liquid called **synovial fluid**, which acts like lubricating oil and flows between the moving ends of bones.

Joint diseases

- Rheumatoid arthritis is another joint problem. Its cause is not clear, but it seems to be due to the body's defense system attacking the joint tissues as though they were invading germs. The joints become red, swollen and painful.
- Gout is caused by a chemical fault in the body. There is too much of the natural chemical uric acid, and it forms crystals in some of the joints, making them swollen and painful.
- Osteo**arthritis** is largely caused by excessive use or wear and tear on a joint. The cartilage in the joints cracks and flakes which leads to pain and stiffness. Osteoarthritis mainly affects the large, weight-carrying joints such as the hips and knees; it sometimes affects the fingers.

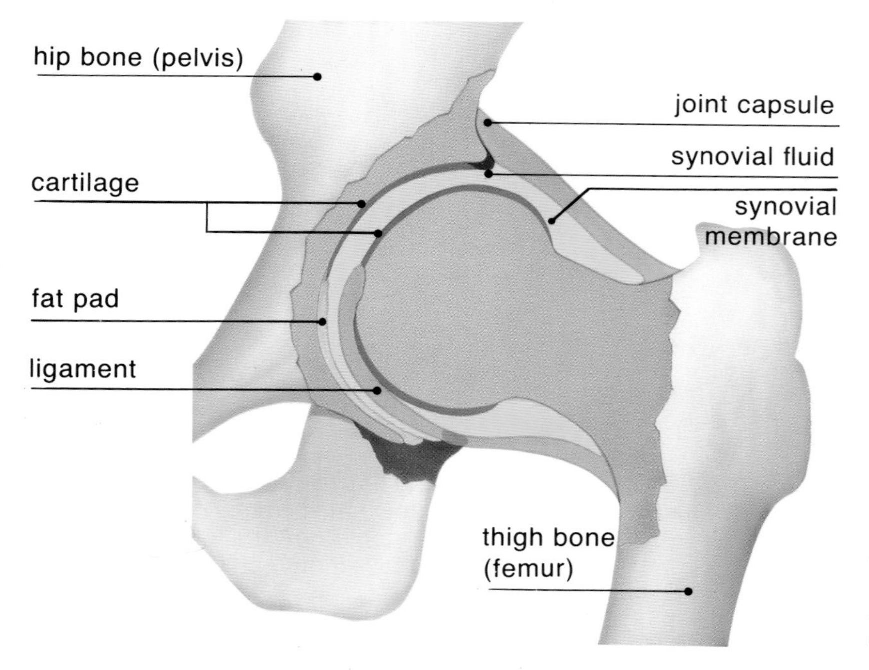

◁ The hip joint, like many movable joints, is made of several layers. Ligaments stabilize the bones, the joint capsule contains the synovial membrane and fluid and smooth cartilage covers the ends of the bones.

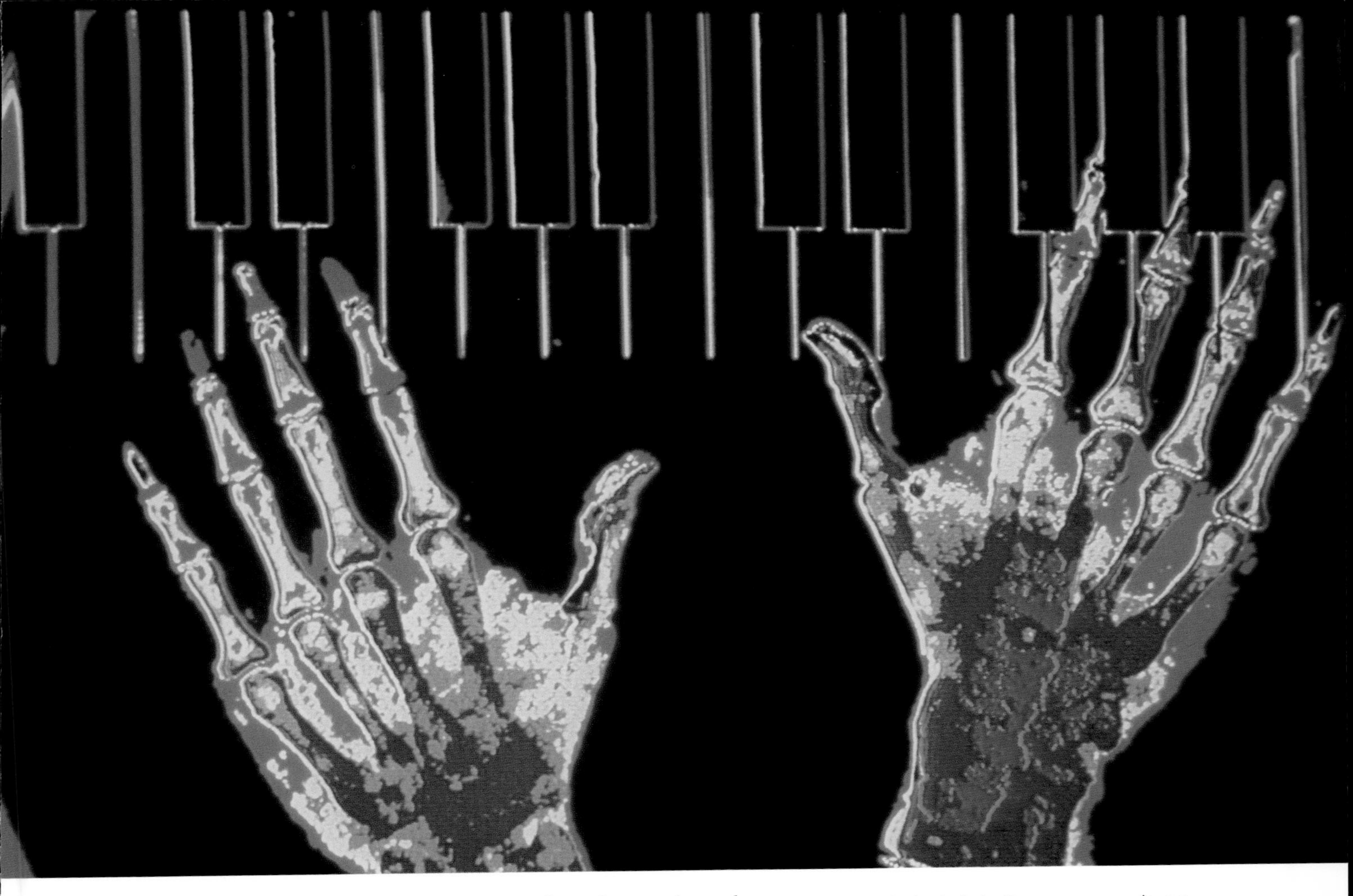

△ In joint diseases such as the various types of arthritis, the tissues of the joint may become red and swollen. This colored X-ray shows how arthritic joints may become stiff, misshapen and painful. Complicated activities like playing the piano become more difficult.

Where bones move over each other, they have a covering of shiny, rubbery cartilage. The cartilage, lubricated by the synovial fluid, is very smooth and helps the bones to slip over each other with hardly any friction. The cartilage, synovial fluid and joint capsule work together as a kind of shock absorber to reduce jarring and knocking as the joint moves.

Friction is a problem, not only in joints, but in any place where two tissues move past each other, such as where a long tendon rubs against a bone. In such places, small capsules containing synovial fluid act as "pads" to reduce wear. These pads are called **bursas**.

In a vehicle, the joints eventually wear out. In the body, joints are formed from living tissue and can repair themselves as they wear. With age or excessive use, however, wear does eventually occur.

Muscles and strength

The human body has three main kinds of muscle – **skeletal muscle, smooth muscle** and **cardiac muscle**.

Skeletal muscle includes the muscles which move the bones of the skeleton. Each one is made of many tiny fibers grouped together into bundles running lengthwise along the muscle. Skeletal muscle is also called striped or **striated muscle** because it looks striped under the microscope. In some muscles these fibers can be more than 12 in (30 cm) long, and the muscle may consist of over 2,000 fibers packed together.

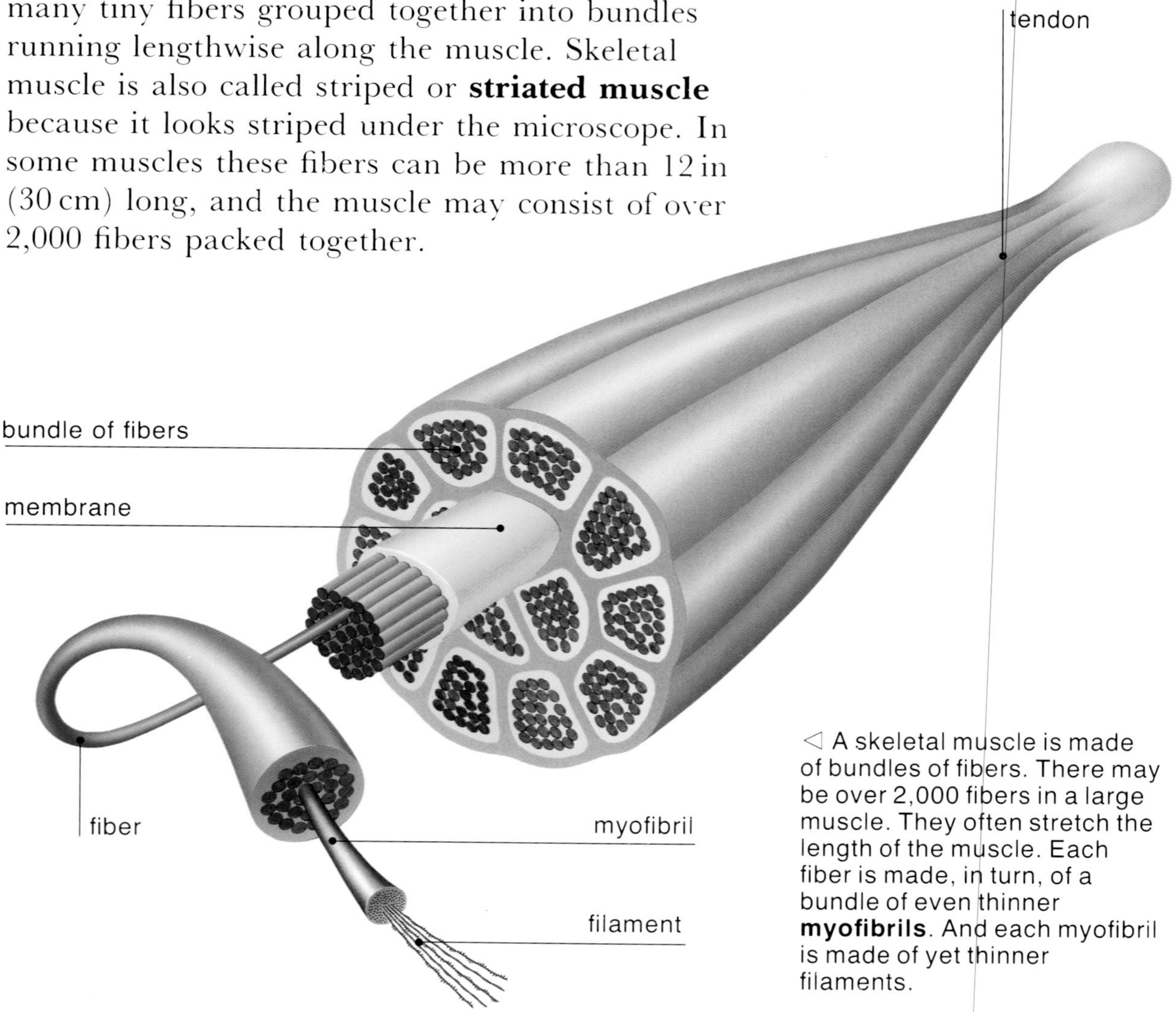

tendon

bundle of fibers

membrane

fiber

myofibril

filament

◁ A skeletal muscle is made of bundles of fibers. There may be over 2,000 fibers in a large muscle. They often stretch the length of the muscle. Each fiber is made, in turn, of a bundle of even thinner **myofibrils**. And each myofibril is made of yet thinner filaments.

Another name for skeletal muscle is voluntary muscle. This is because we can make a conscious decision to make this type of muscle shorten (contract) – in other words, we can move it voluntarily. The other types of muscle are largely under automatic control and we cannot make them move when we want them to.

Smooth muscle is found in internal organs like the digestive system, the blood vessels and the glands. Unlike skeletal muscle, it is not connected to bones. Instead, smooth muscle forms tubes, pouches or sheets, which contract to move their contents. Food is pushed from the mouth down into the stomach by smooth muscle in the wall of the **esophagus** – see page 44.

The third type of muscle is cardiac muscle, or myocardium. This forms the walls of the heart. It contracts about once every second, more often when the body is active, and its movements squeeze blood out of the heart and around the body. Many other muscles work only for a limited time and then become tired or "fatigued." Cardiac muscle never tires – if it did, the heart would stop, and life would cease.

▽ Under a light microscope, bands or stripes (striations) can be seen in skeletal muscle. This effect is produced by the lining up of two types of chemicals (**actin** and **myosin**) within the fibers. The darkest band is where these chemicals overlap.

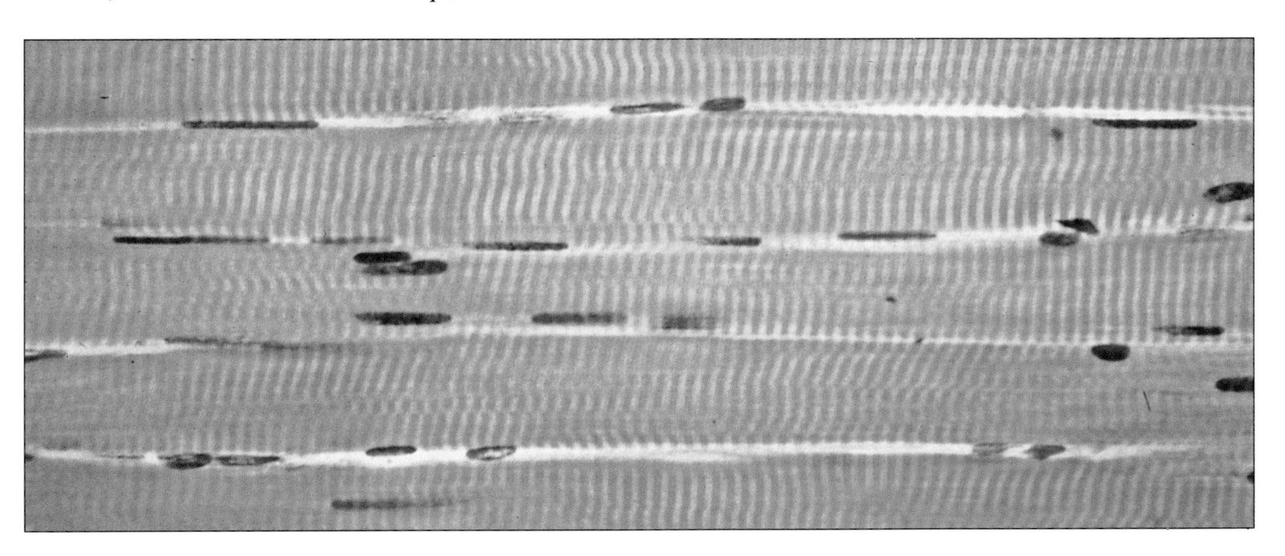

The chemical powerhouse

Muscles work only by shortening; this is called contracting. It means muscles can only pull, they cannot push. Many muscles are arranged in pairs. One pulls one way and the other pulls the opposite way. As one muscle contracts, its partner relaxes and so is stretched (see page 30).

Muscles are controlled by tiny electrical messages sent along nerves from the brain. The messages tell the muscle when to contract, by how much, and for how long. The nerves join a muscle at special microscopic junctions called **motor end – plates**, which lie on top of the muscle fibers. When a message arrives from the brain at a motor end - plate, it triggers the release of a chemical messenger called acetylcholine. This sets off chemical and electrical reactions in the muscle itself, starting the process of contraction.

Muscle fibers are made up of bundles of myofibrils, which are in turn made of protein

Cramp

Cramp is when a muscle contracts spasmodically and involuntarily, pulling hard and feeling tense, knotted and painful. It may occur when you are doing an activity which your muscles are not used to. For example, swimming with the feet pointed backward may cause cramping in the calf muscles. Cramp may be due to a build-up of **lactic** acid, a chemical produced in the muscle during contraction (see page 28).

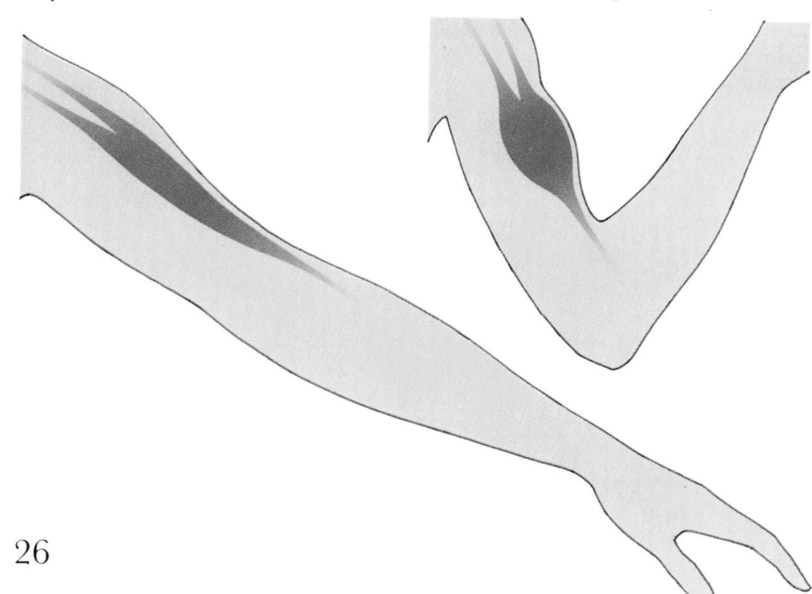

◁ When a muscle contracts, it shortens and also becomes fatter. You can show this by bending up your arm at the elbow. The **biceps** muscle in the top of your upper arm will bulge more and more as it shortens.

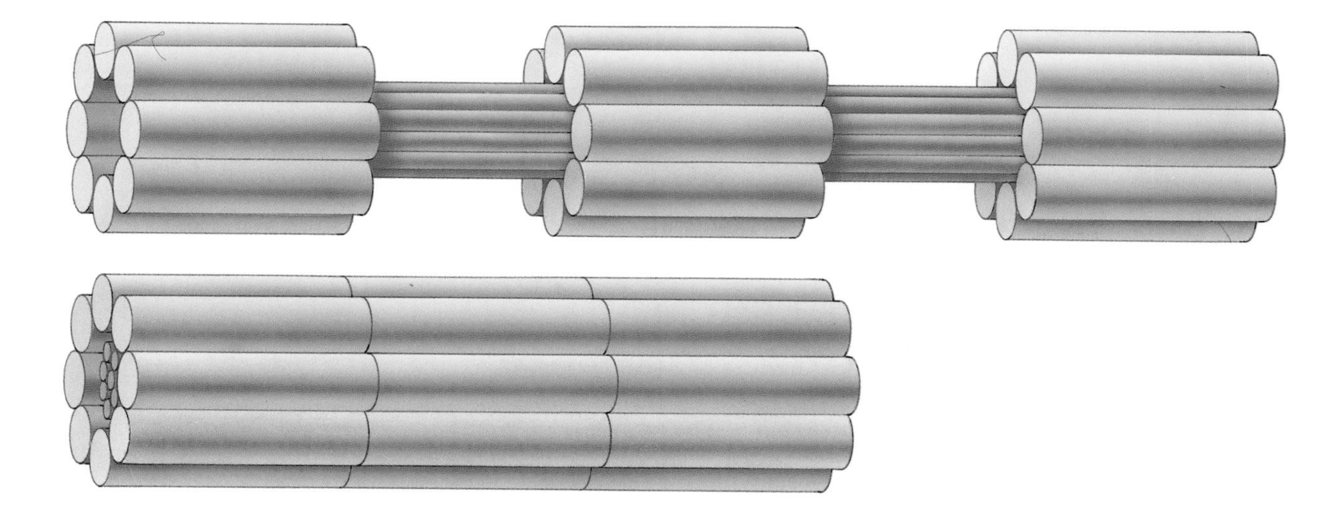

filaments (see page 24). There are two types of protein filament – thicker ones called myosin, and thinner ones called actin. When the chemical and electrical changes begin in the muscle, the thin actin filaments slide in between the thick myosin filaments and the muscle becomes shorter. The filaments grip on to each other partly as a result of the chemical reactions which take place and partly due to "teeth" along their surfaces.

In fact, each muscle fiber is either contracted or not contracted. The more fibers which receive messages to contract, the shorter the muscle becomes, and the stronger its pull. When the messages to contract stop arriving at the muscle, the chemical reactions between actin and myosin stop, and the filaments can be pulled away from each other. In other words, the muscle relaxes.

△ In this diagrammatic view of part of a muscle, the thicker myosin filaments are arranged in groups around the thinner actin filaments. In a relaxed muscle (top), there are gaps between the myosin groups. This causes the light and dark banding seen in the muscle under a light microscope (see page 25). When the muscle contracts, the myosin slides along the actin to shorten the muscle (bottom).

Muscles need fuel

Like any machine, the human body needs a fuel supply. The body has three types of energy-giving fuel, which it obtains from the food we eat. One fuel is **glucose**, a type of sugar. This chemical is found throughout the body, including the blood and the muscles. It is instantly available for work.

A second type of fuel, glycogen, consists of thousands of glucose units joined together. This medium-term energy store is found in the muscles and the liver. As glucose units are required, they are broken off the ends of glycogen and transported in the bloodstream.

The third type of fuel, fat, is a long-term store of energy. When needed, it is broken down into smaller units and carried in the blood to the muscles. This is a long process, and fat is normally

used only when other fuels run low.

The energy in these three fuels is converted into **ATP**, the body's "energy molecule." ATP is found in all cells. As it gives up its energy to power a reaction, ATP is changed to a similar molecule, **ADP**. The ADP is then converted back to ATP using energy from one of the fuels (such as glucose) and is ready to drive another reaction.

Inside muscle fibers, energy is made available by a two-part chemical cycle. The first part does not need oxygen (it is anaerobic) and produces lactic acid as a waste product. This part of the cycle is very fast, but inefficient. It can be used for short, powerful bursts of muscle power such as sprinting. As lactic acid builds up, the muscles begin to ache and cramp and fatigue set in.

The second part of the cycle uses the products of the first part and also oxygen (it is aerobic). It is slower but more efficient and produces only water, heat and **carbon dioxide** as waste products. This aerobic part of the cycle is used for most muscle power.

▽ Exercise means that waste products from the chemical reactions in muscles build up in the body. We pant to remove the excess carbon dioxide (and to absorb extra oxygen), and we sweat more to remove excess heat.

The muscle network

▽ Here are some of the muscles in the shoulder and upper arm. Each one is a certain shape, depending on the type of movement it has to produce.

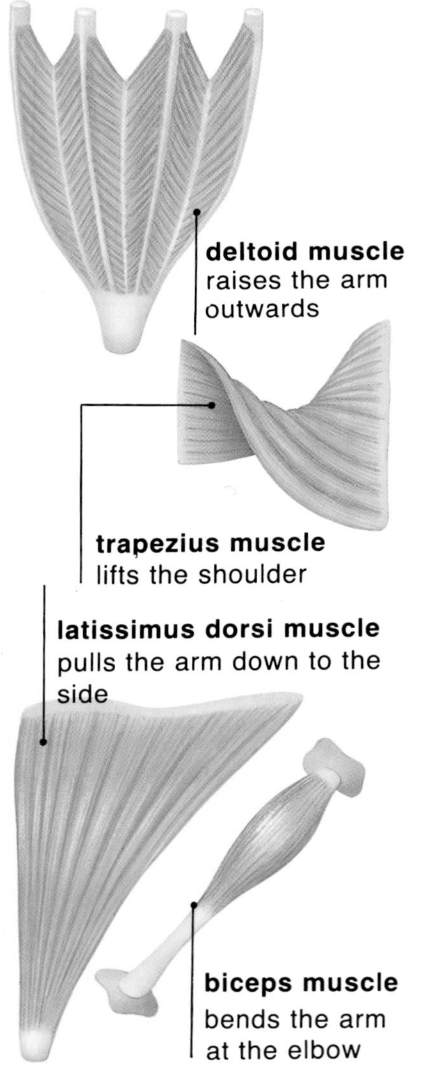

Not all muscles are what we think of as the typical "muscle" shape, wider in the middle, and tapering at each end to a rope-like tendon. Some muscles are extremely long and thin, some are flat and sheet-like, others are triangular or arranged in thick blocks. The shape of the muscle depends on which parts of the body it must move, and where the most efficient line of pull is located.

Muscles often have to work together as a team. As you swing your arm in a circle, dozens of muscles in your arm, shoulder, neck and chest are involved in the movement. Each muscle contracts or relaxes by the right amount to make your movements smooth and coordinated.

How does the brain cope with such a complicated system? Each muscle contracts when instructed to do so by nerves from the brain, called motor neurons. When we are born, there are many motor neurons going to each muscle fiber. As we learn skills like walking and talking, these connections are reduced until a group of muscle fibers is controlled by just one motor neuron.

Each motor neuron is in contact with 1,000s of others, so there is a huge network of control. Muscles such as those in the hand, which perform delicate movements, have only a few fibers in each group to give very "fine" control. Large, powerful muscles, such as those in the leg, have many fibers in each group. This means fewer motor nerves go to that muscle and as a result it is under "coarser" control.

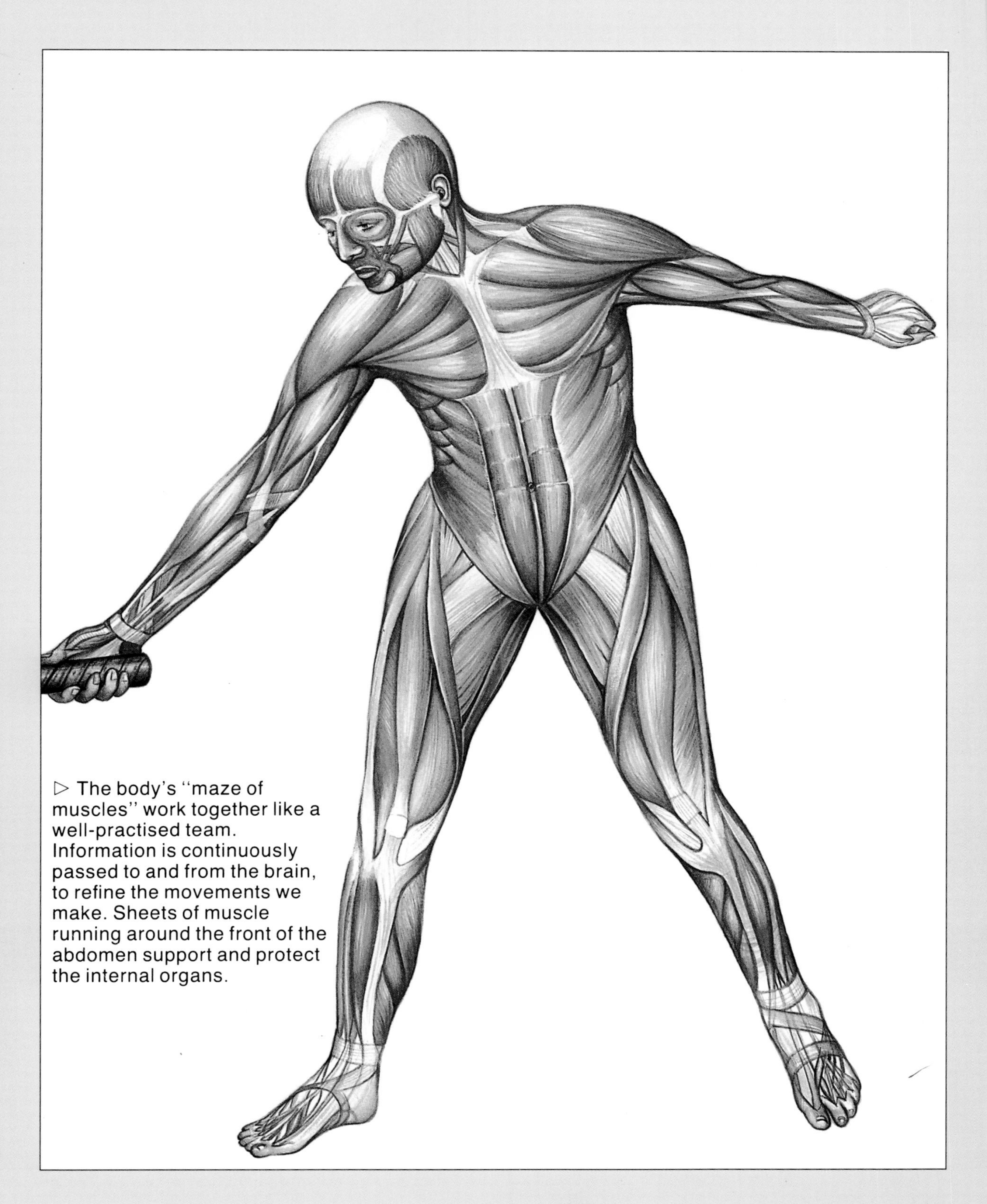

▷ The body's "maze of muscles" work together like a well-practised team. Information is continuously passed to and from the brain, to refine the movements we make. Sheets of muscle running around the front of the abdomen support and protect the internal organs.

Bones as levers

△ Giant cranes like these work along the same principles as your bones and muscles. A strong cable pulls on the jib (lifting arm) of the crane to raise it. In the same way, your upper-arm muscles pull on your forearm to lift it. These cranes have secondary jibs at the top – just as you have a wrist.

The bones of the body, especially those in the limbs, work like a series of levers. The science of mechanics says that a lever has three features. There is a power source which moves the lever – this is the force. There is the object to be moved, such as a weight to be lifted – this is the load. And there is a point of anchorage about which the lever swings or pivots – this is the fulcrum.

There are three main types of lever. First-class levers have the fulcrum between the force and the load, like a pair of scissors, or a nodding head. Second-class levers have the load between the force and fulcrum, like a pair of nutcrackers, or standing on tip-toe. Third-class levers have the force between the load and the fulcrum, like the lifting arm of a crane, or the arm of a person.

Muscles also use another principle of levers. A small movement of the force near the fulcrum, produces a large movement of the load some distance from the fulcrum. You can see this as you bend your elbow. The muscles in your upper arm, connected to your forearm, contract by only a few inches. Yet a weight in your hand moves through over 12 in (30 or 40 cm).

Muscles at rest seem to be soft but are in fact kept in "tone" by continuous small messages from the brain. Some muscles remain tense for long periods, such as those that keep us upright. This is possible without fatigue because different bundles of fibers in the muscle contract in turn, allowing others to rest for a while.

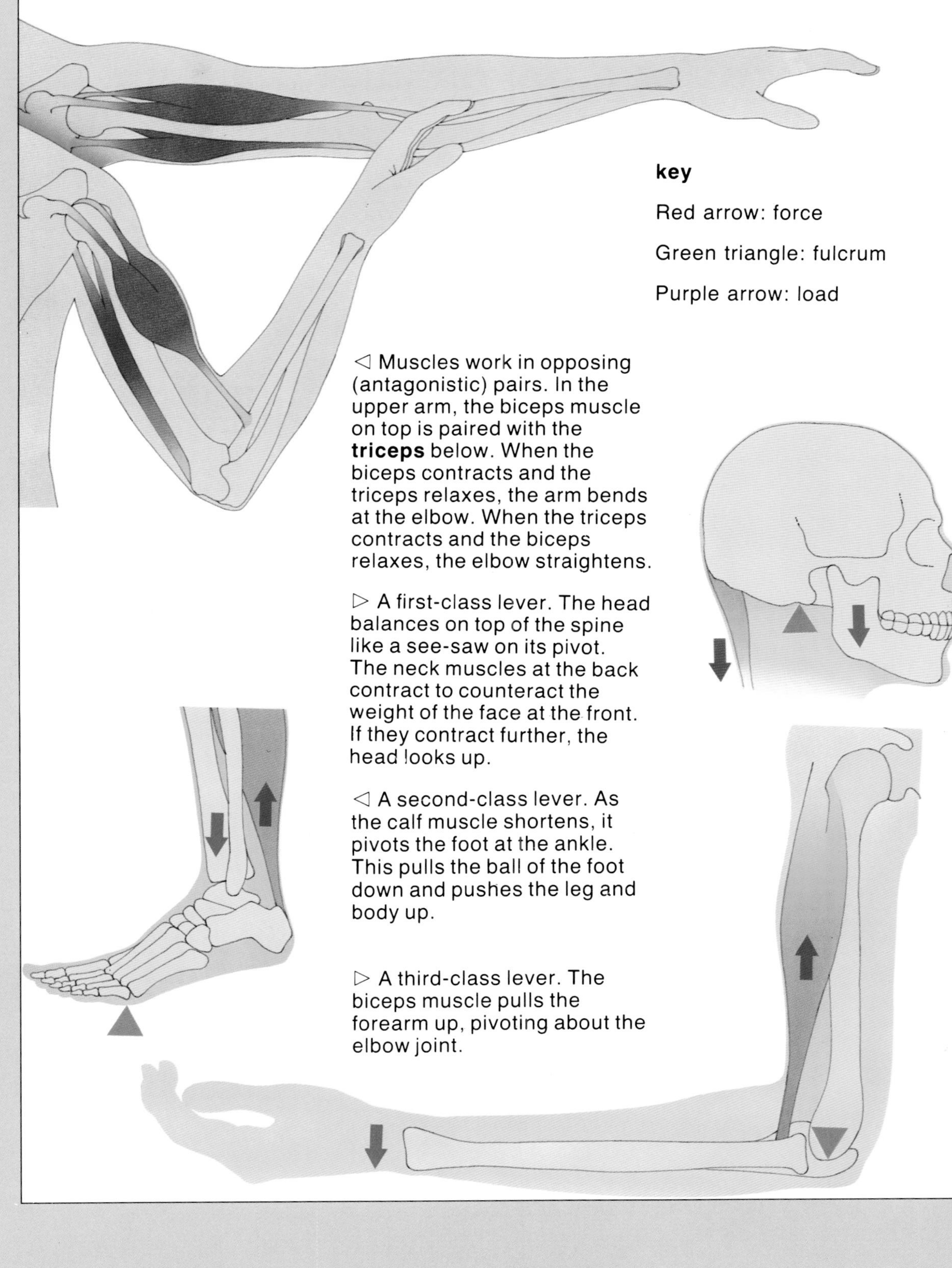

◁ Muscles work in opposing (antagonistic) pairs. In the upper arm, the biceps muscle on top is paired with the **triceps** below. When the biceps contracts and the triceps relaxes, the arm bends at the elbow. When the triceps contracts and the biceps relaxes, the elbow straightens.

▷ A first-class lever. The head balances on top of the spine like a see-saw on its pivot. The neck muscles at the back contract to counteract the weight of the face at the front. If they contract further, the head looks up.

◁ A second-class lever. As the calf muscle shortens, it pivots the foot at the ankle. This pulls the ball of the foot down and pushes the leg and body up.

▷ A third-class lever. The biceps muscle pulls the forearm up, pivoting about the elbow joint.

The versatile spine

The backbone (spine) is central to almost any movements the body makes. It is involved in balance, holding up the arms and head in the correct positions. It anchors the muscles of the limbs, by way of the limb girdles (see page 18). The spine also acts as a spring, to store energy. If you jump up, the spine straightens as you use the energy stored in the "spring." As you land, the "S"-shaped spine bends slightly and stores energy.

The body can bend and twist in almost any direction. A healthy, supple spine allows the body to bend foward almost double. These movements are carried out by layers of muscles running alongside the spine and across and around the trunk. The variety of movement is possible because the spine consists of individual bones, called vertebrae (see page 14). Between the vertebrae are flexible pads of cartilage called intervertebral disks. Each two vertebrae can move only a little, but together they allow the whole spine to move a lot. The vertebrae and their disks are held together strongly by layers of ligaments.

Back problems

- **Lumbago** is a pain in the lower back, sometimes dull and aching, or sharper with movement. It has many causes, including muscle and or ligament strain.
- **Sciatica** is a sharp pain that often seems to shoot from the buttock down one leg, perhaps even to the toes. It is often caused by a:
- **Slipped disk**, when a portion of the jelly-like center of a disk squeezes out and presses on one of the nerves (such as the sciatic nerve) running near to it.

▽ The spine can bend forward (below left), sideways (center) and also twist along its length (right).

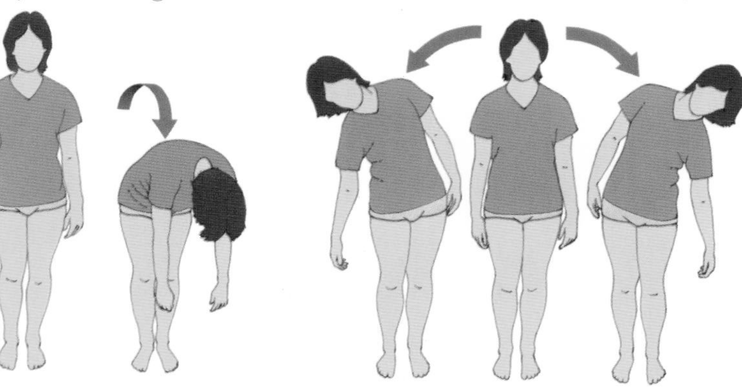

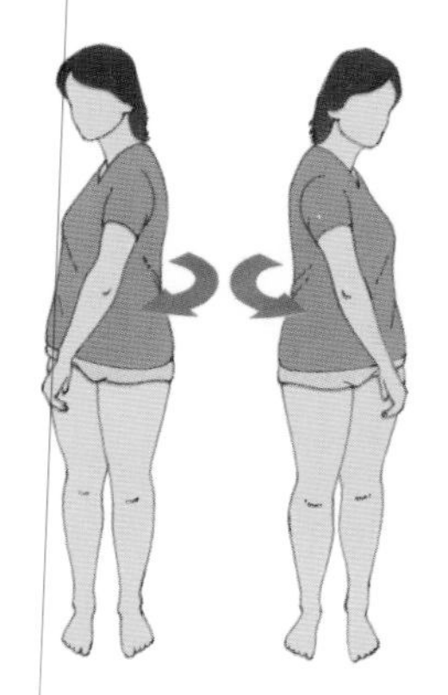

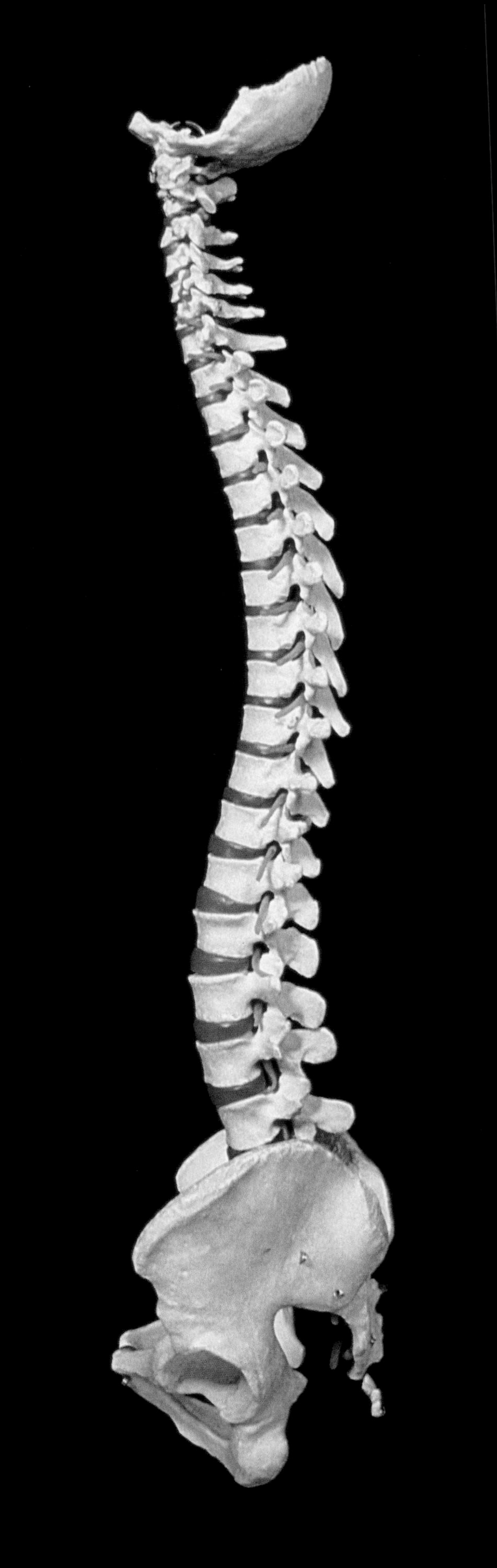

△ As the spine flexes, the disks of cartilage in the intervertebral joints become squeezed on one side and wider on the other.

◁ In this photograph of the spine from the side, the cartilage disks are shown in gray and the nerves running from the spinal cord are in brown. At the top is the base of the skull; at the bottom is part of the hip bone (pelvis).

Facial muscles

▷ Many subtle moods and emotions are conveyed by the movements of the face. How does this man "look?" Is he pleased, or slightly worried?

Humans do not always communicate by speech. Slightly raised eyebrows can indicate doubt. Raised further, they show surprise. A wrinkled nose may mean a bad odor. Sticking out the tongue can convey a horrible taste. A change of just a few millimeters in the angle of the mouth can turn a smile into a frown.

These are only a few of the dozens of facial expressions we use every day, mostly without thinking. The movements of the face are made possible by more than 30 facial muscles. Many of these muscles are anchored to the inside of the skin at one end and to the skull at the other end. Some are fixed to the skin at both ends, while some are anchored to other muscles.

Some of the facial muscles are small, but vitally important. Muscles in the eyelids contract to carry out a blink, bathing the eye with fluid and washing off dust and germs. They may do this more than 20,000 times each day!

Numerous muscles control the lips and cheeks, to form the shapes we need for clear speech. These muscles are well supplied with nerves from the brain, and their control is very finely tuned so that we can make exactly the sounds we want. Most of the time, we do not have to concentrate on this since we learn such movements over many years. We become so well practised that we can spend more time thinking about what to say.

△ Here are just some of the many muscles in the face. Curved muscles run around the eyes and lips. As they contract, they close off these "openings" in the face.

▽ These four facial expressions are produced by muscles contracting. Practise in a mirror. How many different expressions can you make?

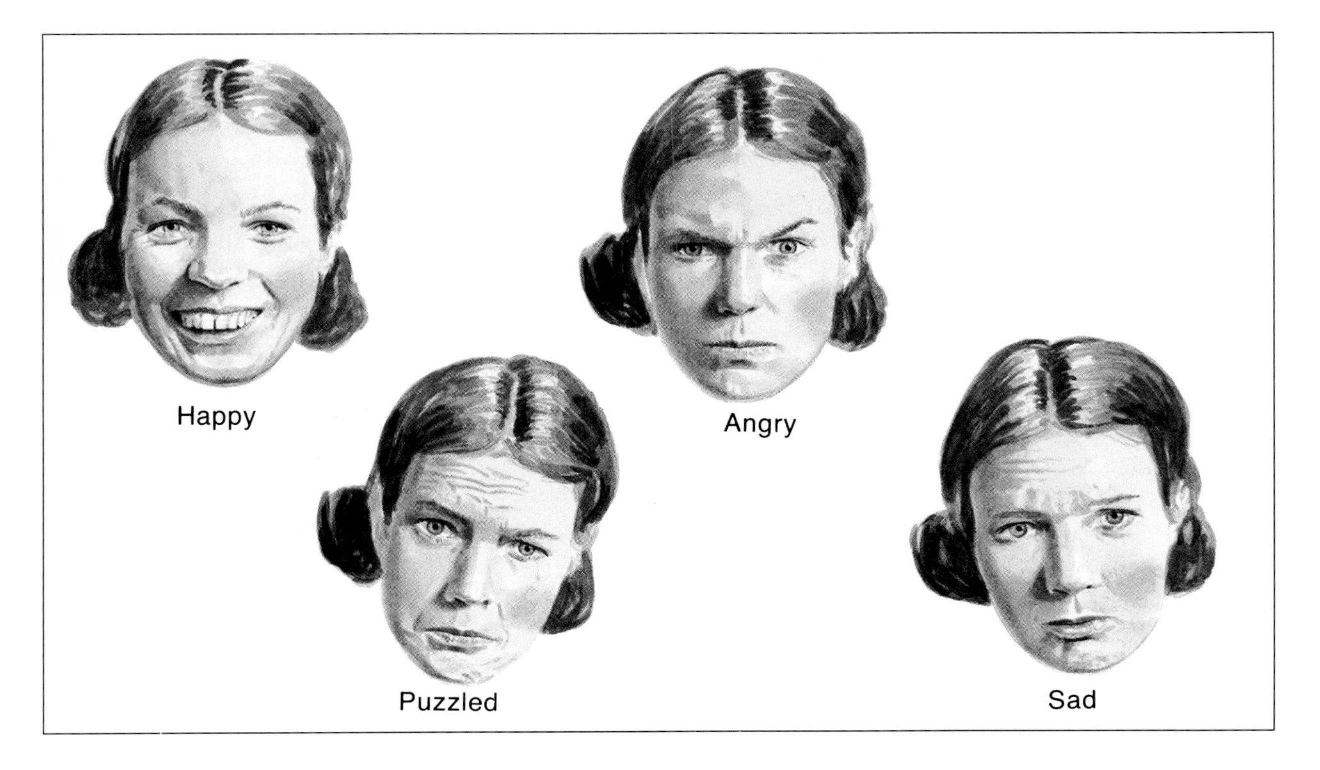

Biting and chewing

One of the most important sets of movements we make is while we eat food. Without the muscles to bite, chew and swallow, we would be unable to take in the energy and nutrients we need to survive.

The lower jaw has two joints just in front of the ears. The joints are not simple hinges, since the lower jaw can move up and down, backward and forward and from side to side. The up-and-down motion allows the front teeth to bite and slice off mouth-sized chunks of food. The other motions help the teeth to squash, crush and grind the chunk of food into a pulp, before it is swallowed.

▽ The different pairs of muscles connected to the lower jaw help it to move in three different directions. This aids thorough chewing of food, which makes it easier to digest. Trying to swallow lumps of badly-chewed food may cause us to choke.

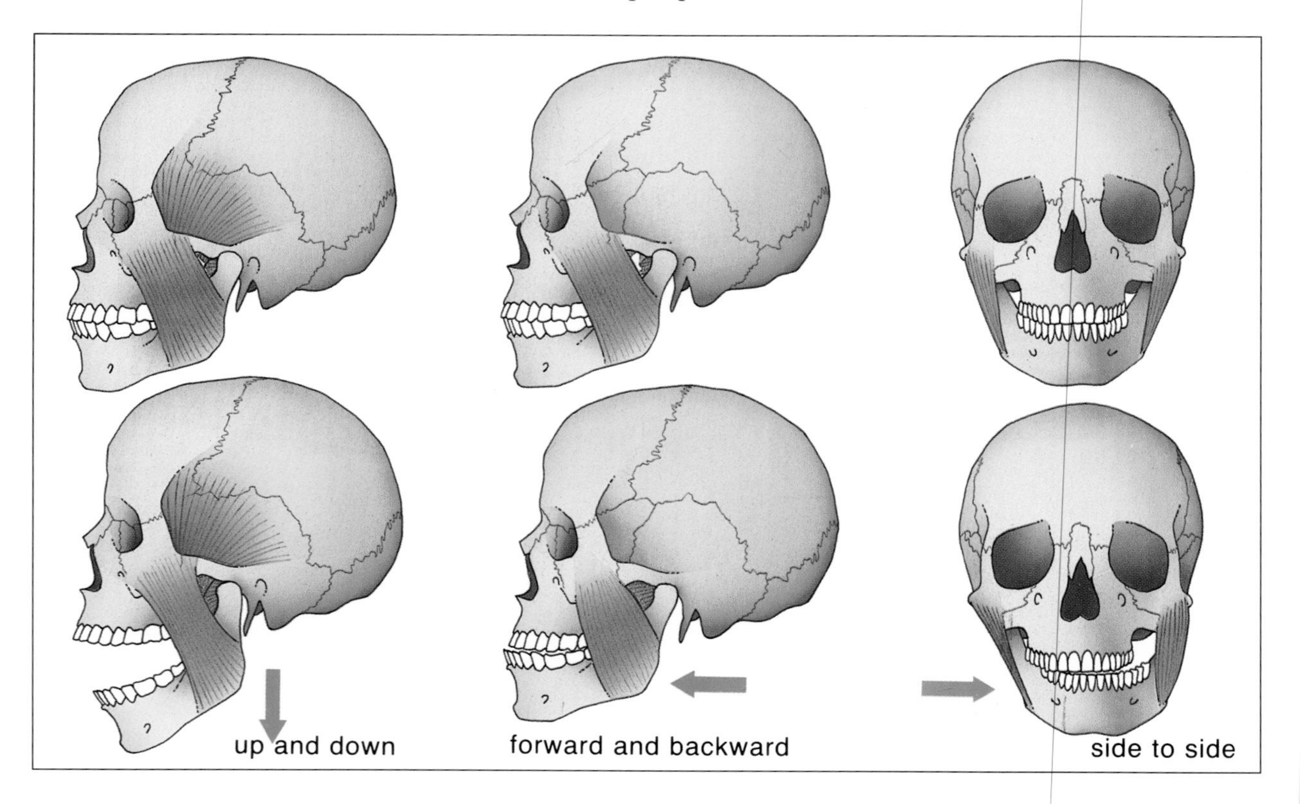

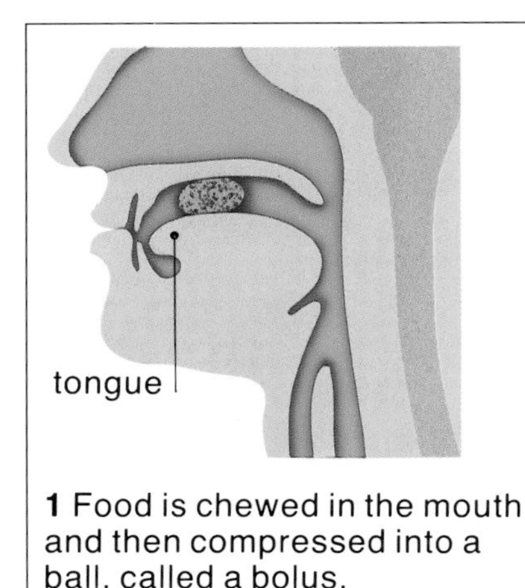

1 Food is chewed in the mouth and then compressed into a ball, called a bolus.

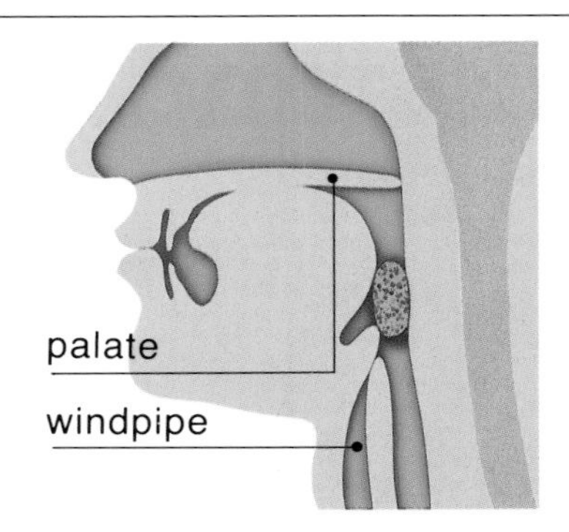

2 The tongue pushes the food to the back of the mouth and down into the top of the throat.

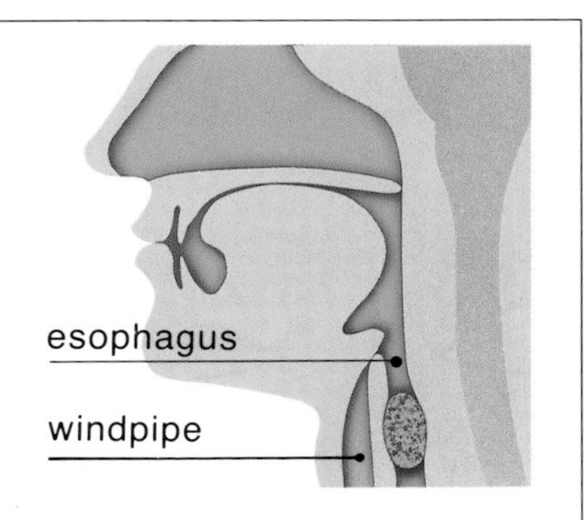

3 As the windpipe closes, the esophagus opens. Muscles in the esophagus wall push the food down to the stomach.

As we chew, the muscles of the lips and cheeks keep the food in the best places for cutting and crushing by the teeth. The tongue, which is almost like one large muscle, also helps in this task by moving and turning over the food.

The jaws are closed by large, flat muscles which run from the lower jaw to the temple region of the skull. You can feel these muscles bulge as you clench your teeth. The force exerted by the teeth is enormous, as we find when we sometimes accidentally bite our cheek during eating.

When chewing is finished, another set of muscles comes into action. These are mainly in the tongue and the roof and floor of the mouth. They work as a team to force food back and down into the esophagus, which leads to the stomach.

Other muscles in the neck enable us to make the movements needed for speech. In the throat, the voice box (**larynx**) makes sounds as air flows out of the lungs and over two small flaps, the vocal cords. The cords are relaxed when we do not wish to make a noise. When their muscles contract, they become tighter and air passing over them makes them vibrate.

△ Humans, and other mammals, have a flap at the back of the mouth which means we can chew food and breathe at the same time. Animals such as reptiles cannot do this. As we swallow, the top of the windpipe closes so that the food does not go down the wrong way into the lungs and cause us to choke.

The complex hand

Engineers have tried many times to build a machine which can copy the human hand. It is amazingly difficult. We can delicately pick a flower petal and hold it gently without damage, or crush it to a pulp.

The fingers and palm of the hand are moved by twenty small muscles within the hand itself, and about fourteen muscles in the forearm, which are joined to the hand bones by more than twenty long tendons. These tendons pass under a large "wrist band" tendon, which runs around the wrist like a thick watchstrap. Hold your wrist and hand flat, look at the inside of the wrist, and then move one of your fingers slightly or curl your fingers into your

▽ Muscles and tendons clothe the hand, running in a criss-cross pattern around each finger. Here the thumb "opposes" the first finger, so that a coin can be held.

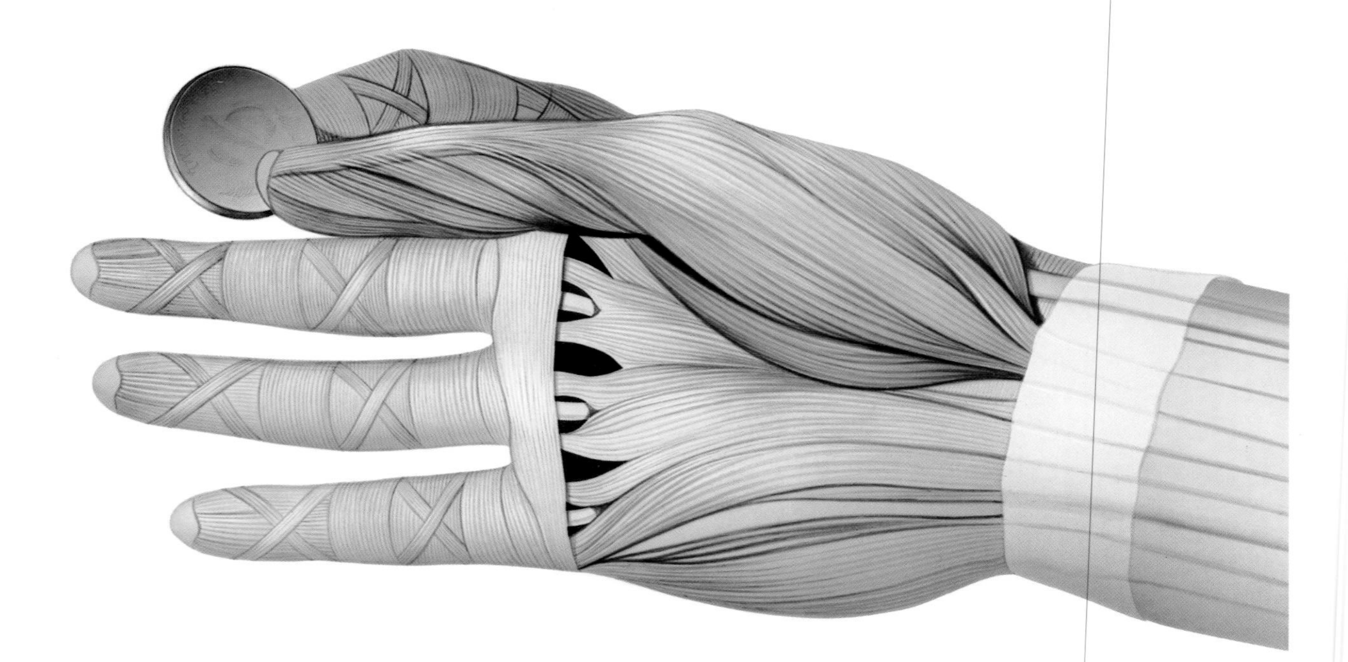

palms. You should see the tendons slide back and forth through the wrist.

Many kinds of joint are found in the hand. The knuckles are mainly hinge joints. The base of the thumb is a complex saddle joint (see page 21) which allows movement in two directions. To a large extent, the thumb accounts for our dexterity. The thumb can touch the tip of each finger in turn and, with the fingers, it can grip strongly in a claw-like fashion. Few other animals have an "opposable thumb" like this. The wrist is made of many squarish bones joined by ligaments, allowing a wide range of movements.

Such a complex system of bones, muscles and joints would be of little use without a good control system. Many nerves run from the brain to the hand and a large part of the brain is dedicated to controlling movements of the hand.

△ Using our nimble fingers, lace-making is one of many intricate skills we can learn. As we practise, the brain gets used to certain patterns of movements so that these become faster and more coordinated. Although the fingers seem to be moving by themselves, the brain is still in control.

Leg power

Most animals about our size have four legs, and many of them can run a good deal faster than we can. We have only two legs, but we can still move quite fast. Top human sports competitors use their legs to leap over a bar 7 ft 10 in (2.4 m) high, jump almost 30 ft (8.9 m) lengthways, and run 100 meters in under ten seconds, at a speed of about 22 mph (35 kph). If your legs could move as fast as those of an ant, you would be able to run at more than 100 mph (160 kph)!

The legs are made on the same basic plan as the arms. But they are not involved with manipulation or dexterity – their functions are power and speed. The legs have much longer, thicker bones than the arms, to give a long stride and take the stresses put on them by the more powerful muscles.

The ankle is similar to the wrist, being made of several block-shaped bones linked together. There are eight bones in the wrist and seven in the ankle. The ankle bones are bigger and stronger than those in the wrist, to bear the weight of the whole body, and to provide the push forward and upward as the foot bends. At the rear of the ankle is the large heel bone (calcaneus). Calf muscles pull on this by way of the achilles tendon, which runs down the back of the lower calf to the rear of the heel.

The muscles in the thighs and calves also help to push blood around the body. As we use our legs, these muscles "massage" blood in the large veins between them. They help to squeeze the blood upward, back to the heart.

Sports injuries

Most sport injuries occur around the joints of the legs. Two of the most common injuries are a sprain and a dislocation.

- A sprain occurs when ligaments around a joint are over-stretched. Often the joint swells up and a bruise forms. Treatment is with a cold compress and rest.
- A dislocation occurs when the bones of a joint are displaced by an injury. Sometimes, ligaments and tendons are torn or a nerve becomes trapped, causing great pain.
- To help prevent these and other sports injuries, it is important to do some gentle "warm up" exercises to prepare the muscles for the hard work to come.

△ A punch can be powerful, but a kick even more so. This martial arts expert shows that the legs are longer and stronger than the arms. One leg is being used to deliver the blow while the other is ready to cushion the body and balance it on landing.

◁ The legs and feet are able to support the body easily during everyday movements. Yet even on a vertical rock face, this climber is able to support and balance the body on the legs. In some climbing movements, the body has to rest on a narrow ledge and all the weight must be carried on the tips of the toes.

Involuntary muscles

Pushing food

Food is moved through the digestive system by the wave-like contractions of peristalsis.

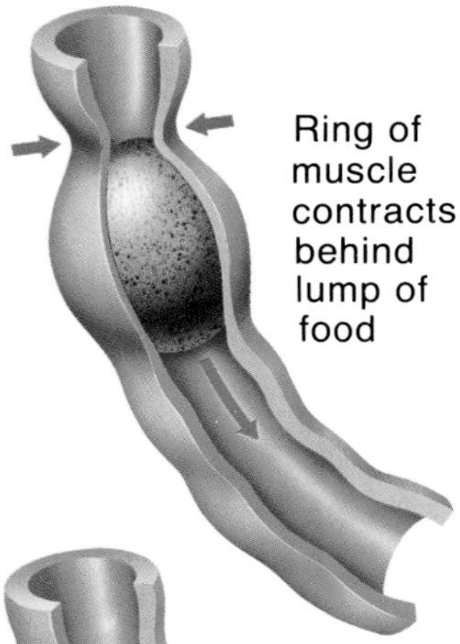

Ring of muscle contracts behind lump of food

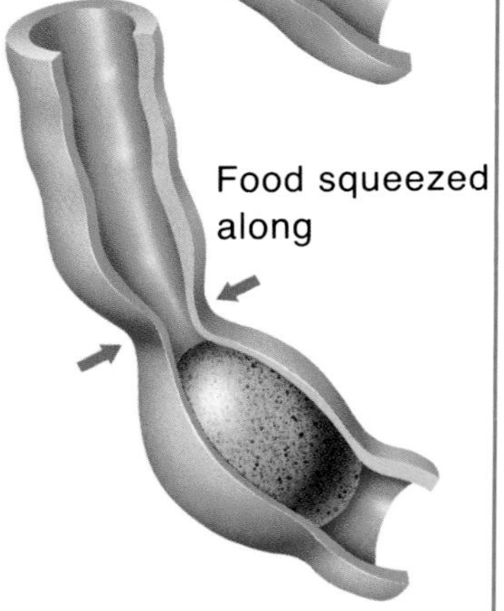

Food squeezed along

Ring of muscle farther along then contracts, so pushing the food even farther. This process continues along the digestive tube.

Many of the muscles in our body are at work all the time, automatically, without us having to think about them. They are contracting and relaxing even when we are asleep. These are the smooth or involuntary muscles of our internal organs, as opposed to the striped or voluntary muscles of the skeleton (see page 24).

Smooth muscle is made up of spindle-shaped cells. Each one has a control center or nucleus, usually seen under the microscope as a dark spot. Smooth muscle may work automatically, but this does not mean that it controls itself. Like skeletal muscle, it is controlled by nerves. The nerves belong to the part of the nervous system called the autonomic nervous system. This takes care of processes like digestion, and also changes the internal size (bore) of blood vessels called arteries, which supply blood to all organs of the body. As an artery narrows, it allows less blood through; as it widens, the blood flow increases. This system controls the flow of blood to the organs, diverting more blood to parts of the body that need it most.

Compared to striped muscle, smooth muscle responds slowly and contracts gently. It usually forms sheets around organs or within their walls. For example, muscle layers in the walls of the esophagus and intestine are circular and longitudinal (lengthwise). The circular muscles contract behind a lump of food to push it along. The longitudinal muscles contract to open the tube again. This process is called **peristalsis**.

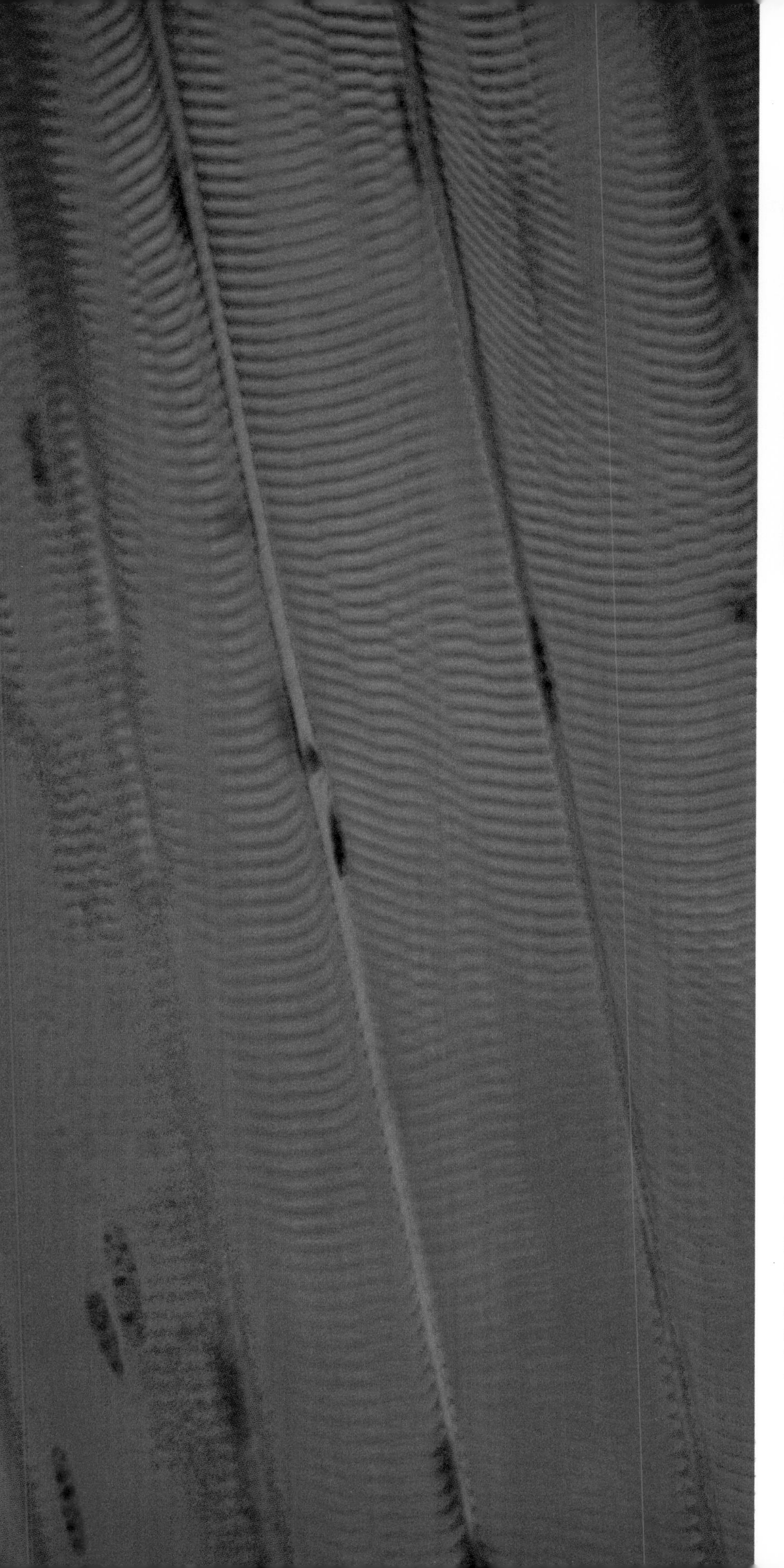

△ Under the microscope, smooth muscle looks quite different from skeletal (striped) muscle. The muscle fibers are shorter and arranged in sheets or blocks. This picture is magnified 150 times.

◁ Skeletal (striped) muscle has characteristic stripes across it when seen under the microscope (see also page 25). It moves the bones of the skeleton, under our conscious control. The brain sends nerve messages to the muscle, the muscle contracts, the bone is pulled – and so the human body moves.

Glossary

Abdomen: the part of the trunk below the ribs.
Actin: chemical found in muscles; with myosin, it forms a sliding "ratchet" mechanism which is the basis of muscle contraction.
ADP: adenosine diphosphate, a body chemical (see **ATP**).
Arthritis: very painful condition caused by inflammation of a joint or joints.
ATP: adenosine triphosphate, a chemical that provides power to run the body. It breaks down into ADP, releasing energy. ADP is then recycled into ATP once more.
Biceps: the large muscle in the upper arm which raises the forearm.
Bursa: small sac containing fluid, which acts as "padding" and reduces friction between moving parts of the body, for instance, where a tendon slides past a bone.
Calcium: mineral in the body that helps in the growth and repair of bones. Also found in teeth, hair and nails.
Carbon dioxide: colorless gas produced as a waste product by the body and removed by the lungs.
Cardiac muscle: special type of muscle which forms the walls of the heart. As it contracts, it pumps blood around the body.
Carpals: eight bones, mostly box-shaped or triangular, inside the wrist.
Cartilage: rubbery, slippery material that lines joints, reducing friction and cushioning the bones.
Cell: the smallest living unit of the body.
Clavicle: long, thin bone running across the front of the shoulder.
Coccyx: tiny "tail" at the bottom of the spine. It consists of several vertebrae fused together.
Collagen: tough, leathery material that strengthens bones.
Cranium: the rounded part of the skull, which surrounds the brain.
Diaphragm: sheet of muscle across the base of the chest (**thorax**), which separates it from the abdomen below. It is important in breathing.
Esophagus: the gullet. Tube through which food is conveyed from the mouth to the stomach.
Femur: the thigh bone; the heaviest and strongest single bone in the body.
Fibula: the thinner of the two bones in the lower part of the leg.
Glucose: a food substance that provides energy to convert ADP to ATP, thus fuelling muscle contraction.
Humerus: the single bone of the upper arm. Its tip forms the elbow, or "funny bone".
Intervertebral disk: disk of cartilage that cushions the vertebrae.
Intestines: long muscular tube in the abdomen in which food is partly digested.
Joint: the connection between bones. Some joints are firmly fixed and rigid; others allow free movement of the bones.
Lactic acid: chemical waste product formed in the muscles. High levels of lactic acid cause muscle tiredness.
Larynx: the voice box. A small box of cartilage, positioned in the neck, containing the vocal cords. It produces sounds as air is forced from the lungs between the vocal cords.
Ligament: tough, ropy material that binds the bones of a joint together.
Mandible: the strong, curved bone forming the lower jaw and chin.
Marrow: soft, fleshy tissue in the hollow center of certain bones of the body. Various blood cells, including red blood cells, are made in the bone marrow.
Maxilla: bone below the

nose, under the upper lip. The two maxilla, one on each side of the face, form the upper jaw.
Motor end plate: tiny, flat plate at the end of nerves in the muscles, which release a chemical that tells muscle fibers to contract.
Muscle: bundle of fibers which contract together when instructed to do so by the nervous system. The muscle causes the movement of bones or other parts of the body.
Myofibrils: strands of thread-like material within muscle fibers, which move together to cause the fiber to shorten or contract.
Myosin: see **Actin**.
Ossification: the process by which the bones of a young person, which are made of cartilage, harden to become bone.
Patella: small, circular, cushion-shaped bone on the front of the knee joint: often called the kneecap.
Pelvis: girdle of bones made up of a pair of hip bones attached to the sacrum, the lower part of the spine.
Periosteum: outer covering or "skin" of a bone.
Peristalsis: wave-like muscular movements of the intestine which move food along during digestion.
Proprioceptors: nerve endings specialized to detect the amount of "stretch" in a muscle or other body part.
Radius: one of the pair of bones in the forearm. The radius is on the same side of the arm as the thumb.
Rickets: disease caused by a lack of vitamin D in children. It causes the bones to become deformed.
Sacrum: lower part of the spine, connected to the pelvis or hip bone. The sacrum consists of five vertebrae.
Scapula: the shoulder blade, a large, shovel-shaped bone at the back of the shoulder.
Skeletal muscle: type of muscle that moves the bones of the skeleton.
Skeleton: the 206 bones that make up the framework of the body.
Smooth muscle: type of muscle found in internal organs.
Spinal cord: large bundle of nerve tissue running down from the brain, protected by the spine.
Spine: the jointed backbone, consisting of 33 bones, joined together so that they support the body, whilst allowing it to bend.
Sternum: the breastbone, a sword-shaped bone joining the ribs at the front of the chest.
Striated muscle: another name for skeletal muscle.
Suture: type of joint where two edges of bones are "knitted" solidly together, allowing no movement – as in the bones of the skull.
Synovial fluid: liquid that lubricates certain joints.
Synovial membrane: thin "skin" inside a joint, which makes the synovial fluid that lubricates the joint movements.
Tarsals: seven bones, mostly box-shaped or egg-shaped, inside the ankle.
Tendon: tough, ropy tissue which connects a muscle and a bone.
Thorax: the chest; upper part of the trunk.
Tibia: shin bone at the front of the lower leg.
Triceps: muscle in the upper arm, which extends the forearm as it contracts.
Ulna: one of the pair of bones in the forearm, on the side opposite the thumb.
Vertebrae: small bones in the back, joined together to make up the spine.

Index

PRINTED IN BELGIUM BY proost INTERNATIONAL BOOK PRODUCTION